<u>BOOTPRINTS</u>

Hobert Winebrenner

BOOTPRINTS

An Infantryman's Walk Through World War II

Hobert Winebrenner
and
Michael McCoy

Camp Comamajo Press

Library of Congress Control Number: 2004095012

ISBN: 0-9759155-0-9

This book does not serve as an all-encompassing history of World War II or of any particular unit. Rather, it is strictly a personal tale of war, autobiographical in nature, as viewed through one man, Hobert Winebrenner's eyes. Constructed almost entirely from his notes and memories, the book may contain unintentional errors in dates, locations, and or details. Although the authors and publisher have made every effort to ensure the accuracy and completeness of information contained in this book, we assume no responsibility for errors, inaccuracies, omissions, and or any inconsistencies herein. Dialogue has been reconstructed to the best of the author's recollections. Any slights of people, places or organizations are unintentional.

… dedicated to our wives and children,
with love forever.

- Hobert and Michael

Acknowledgements

Thanks to all the family members of the soldiers of the 3rd Battalion, 358th Infantry, who contributed pictures and information: Mike Arthur, Gretchen Bacon, Francis Bealke, Jane Bulger, Sandra Kerr, Mary Hoesch, Ruth Hohman, Wade Inman, Carla Calvert, Ernie Rezac, Naomi Rother, Eveline Simpson, Helen Kutach, Jerry Wiley, Tom Hill, John Marsh, Jr., Herbert Roeglin and Harold Wooderson.

Thanks to those old soldiers still around, who so graciously volunteered their stories and guidance: Don Benedict, Richard Bulger, Amon Hartwick, John Mateyko, Allan McInnis, Howard Pemberton and Bob Smith.

Thanks to the *Albion New Era* newspaper, for giving us a start. And special thanks to Barb Crozier, who organized our ramblings into a manageable form.

Thanks to Tyler Alberts, head of the 90th Documentary Project, whose contributions have proved invaluable. Now some six years in the making, his forthcoming offering promises to change the face of war documentaries forever.

Thanks to Ann Wintrode, for her discerning eye.

Thanks to our families—parents, wives, children and grandchildren. You make each day alive and new. Without your love and support, we would be nothing.

Thanks to our Lord and Savior, Jesus Christ. Through Him, all things are possible.

- Hobert and Michael

Preface

Your aged next door neighbor, the old man in front of you at the store, the elderly gentleman across the aisle at church, another body buried in the local cemetery—what do we owe these men, our fading World War II generation? In short, a debt we can never repay.

Heroes live amongst us. Quietly patriotic, most ask for nothing, but respect. Yet, they are due so much more.

I've tried to take their offering personally. Long ago, they fought for and won freedom for me. Without their selfless sacrifice, I surely would not live the life I do today.

Several years ago, I began tracking them down, not only to show my appreciation, but also to learn more of their struggles. The journey has proved nothing short of amazing.

One local veteran in particular caught my attention. I'd heard only bits and pieces of his tale, but still enough to know it was special. Late one rainy weekday afternoon, we settled down at his kitchen table to revisit his war. Initially, he glossed over difficult details and spoke only of generalities. But as he became more familiar with my face, more comfortable with my demeanor, he dug deeper.

As if pulled back in time, his eyes strained, his voice cracked. His memory painted such vivid pictures, I almost felt as though I'd been by his side, in a front line foxhole. Throughout the course of the session, he excused himself from the table several times, overcome with emotion. Within him, war buddies, long since gone, lived forever on.

In parting company that day, his wife, Marian informed me that her husband had just revealed more in the last few hours, than he had in the previous sixty years combined. I felt honored by his forthright candor. And he seemed pleasantly surprised to find a young man so genuinely interested. On some base level, we connected that day.

Hobert Winebrenner had spoken of his desire to leave something behind for his children, grandchildren and those yet to come—not so much about him, but about those with whom he served. "The finest men in the world," he often beamed.

I concurred. Others should know of his struggle—their struggle to defeat evil. I soon realized that this story called to a larger audience. To do it justice, a book needed to be written.

I believed it in my head and felt it in my heart. How different would my life be had men like Hobert refused to stand up and fight? I had not suffered or sacrificed as they. Yet today, I breathe the same air and enjoy the same rights. The very least I could do was to bring another of their stories to light.

So began our two years of kitchen table summits. We sorted through Hobert's war step by step, bit by bit, bullet by bullet. We rehashed, reworked and rewrote, almost ad nauseam. Hour upon hour, I listened while he laughed, cried and prayed.

We attempted to track down old army pals, only to find most already gone. And with Hobert at age eighty-two, the endeavor often seemed like a race against time. But at long last, the finish line—our mission is complete. Please enjoy.

Thanks For Reading,

Michael McCoy

Contents

Chapter 1

Before The Storm

Albion, Indiana to Bristol, England

Then Along Came The War
Born and raised in Middle America, I grew up in tiny Merriam, Indiana. When I graduated from Wolf Lake High School in 1940, I knew little of the greater world at large.

It was a different era, a simpler time. If you got in with a good company, you most likely stayed there for life. Shortly after graduation, I did just that, landing a job with GE in Fort Wayne. My future looked bright.

Along another line, my cousin dated a girl from my high school class. At the time, she attended nurse's training at St. Joseph's Hospital, also in Fort Wayne. He asked me one day, "How'd you like to come over to the hospital with me and maybe meet a nice girl?"

That was the first time I laid eyes on my future wife, Marian. She hailed from Chicago, but was in Fort Wayne to learn the art of nursing. We dated for several months and became quite close.

Good job—great girl, life couldn't be better. But then,

1

along came the war. Of course, it changed everything. I was taken in July of 1942, as part of Noble County's largest draft group. Over eighty of us gathered as directed at the courthouse in nearby Albion. Soon-to-be soldiers and their well-wishing families packed the square and surrounding streets. We assembled on the east side and marched to the train station in one column, four men wide. All aboard! Destination World War II!

Down To The Dustbowl

From Camp Perry, Ohio, I traveled to Camp Wolters, Texas for basic training. Dusty, dry, hot and hard is how I remember it—certainly no picnic. Several others from my home draft group, including a pal named Bud Wysong, followed the same path. Familiar faces eased the difficult transition.

Hobert Winebrenner and Bud Wysong
Camp Wolters, Texas - 1942

I also struck up a fast friendship with a soldier from Bellevue, Ohio–Bob Smith. By coincidence, he too dated a girl named Marion, only hers was spelled with an "o" instead of an "a." On a whim, we journeyed to nearby Mineral Wells and found what we were searching for in the back room of a run-down tavern. It was a rough looking chain smoker, armed with a tattoo needle, who conducted business from two wooden chairs on a dirt floor. We patiently waited our turn, while the artist wrapped up his rendition of some sort of bird on a young woman's upper thigh.

Bob Smith with a BAR, and Hobert Winebrenner
Camp Wolters, Texas - 1942

When our time arrived, we fell short of the purchase price. Thankfully, this guy agreed to take what we had and got right to work. He used the same needle on us all, but we didn't think anything of it. In 1942, "cross contamination" was not part of the common vernacular. In less than an hour, two flat broke, yet smiling young soldiers emerged with "Marian" and "Marion" tattooed on their respective right forearms. That was love! Now marked, there was no turning back. We were in these relationships for the long haul.

Officer Material?

Bob and the rest of my outfit soon left Camp Wolters for North Africa, but I stayed put. Those in charge wanted me to help train the next incoming unit. Once finished, I'd move onto Officers Candidate School (OCS). They apparently saw something in me of which I wasn't aware. Per orders, I first completed my time at Wolters and then reported to Fort Benning, Georgia for a 12-week training course.

Hobert Winebrenner, Willis Winters, Joe Wendling
OCS – Fort Benning, Georgia

At the beginning of my eleventh week, the major in charge summoned four classmates and me into a meeting. The small group included a best friend, Joe

Wendling from Emmaus, Pennsylvania. Our commander presented us each with two options. For one, we could finish our stint there and become second lieutenants in a matter of weeks. On the surface, that didn't sound too bad. If nothing else, that late into our course work, we all expected as much. Or secondly, we could accept staff sergeant ratings and report immediately to Fort Sill, Oklahoma, an artillery training school. Once there, we would instruct artillery officers in the proper use of infantry weapons.

We all chose the latter without thinking twice. Second lieutenant was no dream job. At that time, their life expectancy rivaled that of the common housefly. The army used them up like toilet paper. Even though we had already purchased our new uniforms with accompanying second lieutenant paraphernalia, the decision wasn't a tough one. We all settled for staff sergeant and hurried to Sill.

Moreover, not being regular army, I paid little mind to rank. You met all kinds in the military. Within the same unit, I came to know incredibly capable officers working hand in hand with those who couldn't match wits with a doorknob. The same could be said for noncommissioned officers (NCOs) and privates. As in life, you just couldn't judge a book by the cover or the worth of a soldier by his stars, stripes or lack thereof.

I wasn't regular army and had no intentions of ever being such. I was a "citizen soldier," there to do a job to the best of my ability. But once it was done, I was going home. The rank of sergeant suited me just fine.

The Good Life At Sill

Besides the lack of enemy gunfire, Sill possessed many amenities. We formed the one and only on-base infantry unit, a heavy weapons outfit. Most days, we taught class—a game of show-and-tell with mortars,

BARs and larger water and air-cooled machine guns. Our audiences included not only artillery officers, but also foreign units.

While at Sill, Joe and I met new friends—Amon Hartwick, Bill Adams and Andy Hoesch. We were all part of the same company and often visited our favorite Lawton watering hole together.

Bill Adams and Andy Hoesch
Fort Sill, Oklahoma – 1943

One memorable night, Amon and I bought some boot-leg whiskey to smuggle into the local picture show. We sipped at it only sparingly throughout and exited after-ward with our faculties still fairly intact. But on our way home, we ran into a couple of unfamiliar second lieu-tenants. They walked in our direction, but were at least a block away when I posed the question to Amon, "You feel like saluting these guys?"

Amon Hartwick and Hobert Winebrenner
Fort Sill, Oklahoma - 1943

He responded with a convincing, "Hell no!"
To avoid them, we cut across the street and stared

intently through store glass. Two grown men, side by side, window-shopped as if there was no tomorrow. Unfortunately, the officers followed.

"What was their problem?" we both wondered. We came to find out they headed a team sent to Sill to specifically study the state of "military courtesy." Wow, that's some bad luck!

They filed a report and the next morning, we found ourselves standing at attention in front of our commanding officer's desk. He was a little, well maybe a lot, excited. For ditching these two, they not only busted us down to corporal, but also assigned each of us a month of extra work details. A little harsh, if you ask me. Yet, we did our time and soon both returned to the rank of sergeant.[1]

After approximately a year, the good life at Sill came to an end. All the privates in our outfit were sorted to the 30th Infantry Division, while the NCOs reported to Camp Bowie, Texas. We sat on the shelf at Bowie, until our time arrived.

A New Home

Unbeknownst to us, D-Day neared. In preparation, entire divisions assembled for transfer to England. From Bowie, we traveled to Fort Dix, New Jersey, assigned to the 90th Infantry Division. They sprinkled us throughout different regiments as prospective casualty replacements. Invasion forecasts spoke of impending doom. Accordingly, those in charge beefed up the number of NCOs within each unit. We were extras or fill-ins. With more than enough sergeants on hand, maybe a few might actually survive.

Amon and I landed in the same outfit, while Joe, Bill and Andy were shuffled elsewhere. But on weekends, the old gang often congregated at the Hoesch house in nearby Darby, Pennsylvania. Wonderful folks, Andy's parents always made us feel welcome. We all enjoyed the home cooking and hospitality, although Bill more than most. After the war, he married Andy's sister, Anita.

Marian and I pondered marriage before my departure for overseas duty. But when I learned casualty estimates eclipsed eighty percent, I thought, why bother. I loved her enough not to saddle her with that burden. Marriage would have to wait for my return from war.

I was assigned to M Company of the 358th Infantry Regiment, 90th Division. We were the heavy weapons outfit for the 3rd Battalion and complemented three rifle companies–"I," "K" and "L." I didn't think too much of my new unit, one way or the other. Moved so many times already, I assumed that this was just another stopping point. Little did I know then, "M" would become my home and its men—my family.

Train Ride To NYC

From Dix, we reported to a staging area called Camp Kilmer. There they administered our final shots and confiscated most of our equipment, excluding clothing and personal items.

The train ride from Kilmer to the dock in New York City was a disaster. Filth abounded throughout the vintage Civil War era railway cars. Not only were the toilets inoperable, many windows wouldn't open.

Yet, mechanical problems topped them all. What was supposed to be a few hours took us nearly an entire day. We spent much of our time idle, on the siding. The boat readied to embark, but we weren't on it. At long last, we arrived. None were happier than I to finally vacate that rolling cesspool.

Across The Pond

In New York City, we shuffled from the train to the docks. Already late, we hastily loaded onto the troop ship. The USS John Erickson was a behemoth, with thousands on board. Construction crews had ripped out the below deck levels and filled them with bunks, six high to a floor. Only a few feet existed between beds. Manufactured of pipe and canvas, they ran the entire length from bow to stern, compartment after compartment. This would be no comfort cruise.

We left port on March 23, 1944, but soon returned.[2] An engine problem required immediate attention. In short, our boat broke. Talk of an enemy submarine pack, trolling the approximate area, also circulated throughout the vessel. Perhaps in response, our group gained mass. Several ships, including destroyers and a baby aircraft carrier, joined our convoy. A few days repair saw us once again on our way to England as part of a newly expanded contingent.

I numbered among the sorriest of land lovers and suffered seasickness almost immediately. It wasn't the slight upset stomach variety, but rather a consistent refunding of all deposits. The vast quantity of men aboard dictated the around-the-clock serving of mess—eight hours each of breakfast, lunch and dinner. Friends brought meals to my bunk, but I kept little down. I attached my helmet to the railing in order to catch the output. To this day, bad memories of pea soup and chocolate bars haunt me.

My absence from boat drill brought our company commander, Captain Marsh, and battalion commander, Colonel Bealke, below deck to see me. In no uncertain terms, they ordered me topside, but I just couldn't go.

"What are you going to do if we get hit?" Captain Marsh questioned. "Don't you want to know how to get into a life boat and be saved?"

"Sir, in this state, I'm going down with the ship," I respectfully returned. They eventually left me alone to my misery. With little room to maneuver, there weren't many important things going on anyway.

Land Ho!

After an extended voyage, our party steamed into the port at Liverpool, England. I could barely walk, let alone carry my gear. Simon Arthur, an Arapaho Indian friend of mine, thankfully helped my pack and me exit the vessel.

Simon Arthur – Camp Barkeley, Texas

We quickly gathered aboard troop trains, which waited at the docks. Again terribly frustrating, the rail ride mimicked the one from Camp Kilmer to New York City. There was as much backing up as moving forward. But we eventually reached our new home, an army camp near Bewdley, England.

Life At Bewdley

Quartering crews set the tents, row after row. They housed twelve to fourteen men per and without bottoms, served more like covers than traditional tents. A folding cot and two blankets were issued to each of us. We were fortunate to still possess our big GI overcoats. Some of those April English nights chilled to the bone.

"Attention to detail" epitomized life at Bewdley. Officers were overly particular about everything, even our eating habits. They went so far as to check our plates to make sure we had cleaned them. After one evening meal of stewed tomatoes, I exited to wash my mess kit. A lieutenant stood at the station and noticed that some of my juice remained. He was part of the Division's original cadre from Camp Barkeley, Texas. I fail to mention his name because I disliked the man immensely. From our first meeting at Dix, we didn't see eye to eye on much of anything. Our exchanges resembled confrontations more than conversations. Yet, he was an officer and I, an enlisted man—enough said.

"Sergeant, get back in there and finish your meal!" he barked.

Although still mindful of proper military etiquette, I deeply desired to try his patience. Accordingly, I answered, "Sir, I've only got a fork and the juice keeps running through the tines." Unimpressed, he coarsely ordered me to get some bread, sop it up and watch my attitude.

A friend, Garold Anderson from Lansing, Michigan, walked behind me. He had a little fat left on his plate and for good measure, a shoestring untied. Lieutenant "Spit-n-Polish" really berated him for that combination. Back to the table we both went. I ate some more bread and covertly poured my juice onto the ground. After Anderson tied his shoe and stuck the fat in his pocket, we were free at last.

*Two Midwestern boys clowning around,
Garold Anderson and Hobert Winebrenner.*

The showers were strictly the open-air variety. Once in, it was a race against the clock. You had to quickly soap and rinse before the water shut down. As with everything else, personal hygiene worked on a limited basis, from the tightest of schedules.

Canvas surrounded the restroom area to serve as makeshift cover. Buckets set in the center of 2 x 4 frames. You just selected the least full pail and conducted your business. Each morning, two limeys in a beat-up tanker truck pulled in to empty the mess. They wore large rubber aprons and gloves for protection. Back in 1940s England, sewage removal lacked technology. One man handed the buckets up to the other, perched atop the tank. He just dumped it in, pail after pail.

Officially, they trucked this waste to a treatment plant and cooked it down to dust, but none of us believed it. We all imagined they drove out into a nearby field and yanked the plug—you know, fertilizer.

We seldom ventured into town, only when allowed. Bewdley was small. Modern advancements had largely passed her by.

I remember only one village pub. Straight-backed chairs accommodated four or five simple tables, scattered about a well-oiled, hardwood floor. A couple of whiskey bottles and one beer pump quietly begged for attention atop a small bar. I silently wondered how much this place had changed over the last two hundred years—probably, not much.

We all ordered beer on my first and last time there. Neither world travelers nor heavy drinkers, we just assumed that British brew resembled ours. When they served us up a glass, thick and dark, at room temperature, it startled us. I'm not sure any of us found the bottom of our pints that day—another cultural lesson learned.

One Step Closer

Beyond Bewdley, we moved to a camp near Bristol, England. Through a letter, I attempted to tell my mother of our location. I understood this to be forbidden, but couldn't resist. Back home near Merriam, Indiana, Bristol Lake lay just behind my parents' farm. By guilefully hinting at a connection, I tried to tie the two together. I really thought I was quite sly, right up until the runner came. The officer in charge of scanning our mail needed to see me, immediately. My clever creation now resembled Swiss cheese. He had sliced out all the geographically descriptive passages to the point that little remained. I assured him that I meant no harm. He let it and me go our separate ways. Mom probably thought a mouse got a hold of that letter.

Most days and many nights, we trained vigorously. We hiked often with full field packs strapped to our backs, twelve to fifteen miles at a time. Stocked complete, they weighed sixty to eighty pounds. No question, we were in top physical shape.

I experienced a memorable encounter, while on a training exercise. I worked on an instrument that measured the difference in elevation between two points. I was sighting it in, when a jeep rolled up and an officer got out. He gave me an "at ease" and casually began to ask a few questions. I told him what we were doing and how things were going, but didn't think much of it. Initially, because he wore a regular field jacket and his jeep was unmarked, I couldn't tell his rank. But when he turned to the side, the stars on his collar caught my attention. That's when I realized, I was speaking to General Bradley. He made the conversation comfortable, as easy as two farmers talking in a field. In the end, he shook my hand and offered some encouraging words about God, America, Mom and apple pie. He also cautioned me not to get too attached, for our time was near.

The invasion approached and we were restricted to camp for final preparations. Only days later, we traveled by rail to the harbor at Cardiff and loaded onto our ship.

The mood was not somber, but quiet. Guys looked inside themselves and reflected on what had been and what was about to be. We all knew this day would come. But when it finally did, I'm not sure any of us were ready. It was time! Our time! The world's time!

Chapter 2

The Landing, D + 2

Utah Beach – Normandy, France

Here We Go!

Once out to sea, our vessel, the SS Bienville, treaded water off the southern coast of England. Officers briefed us on the situation. We poured over maps, charts and objectives. The calendar read June 6, 1944, and Americans were already landing and dying on Normandy's beaches. We crossed the English Channel on June 7.

Through an earlier letter from Bewdley, I had asked my mother to send me a snap-bladed knife. It arrived in short order and I sharpened it to a razor's edge. It somehow unlocked and opened, while I lay in my rack that night. When I reached into my pocket to move it, the exposed blade sliced my hand to the bone.

So entered Richard "Doc" Bulger into my life. Born and raised in Pittsburgh, he knew from a very early age that he wanted to be a physician. He graduated from the University of Pittsburgh Medical School on June 15,

1941, and married his wife, Theresa, the very next day. Upon completion of a one-year, rotating internship at Western Pennsylvania Hospital, Doc joined the Army.[1] He served as our Battalion Surgeon.

Captain Richard "Doc" Bulger
3rd Battalion Surgeon, 358th Infantry

I asked nervously, "Doc, do you think you could numb the area some before you stitch it up?"

He smiled wryly and answered me with the question, "Now who's the doctor here?"

Doc Bulger called them like he saw them, never one to over dramatize a situation. For an anesthetic, he offered me a couple of aspirin, then commenced sewing. He stitched it up in no time. His handiwork appeared top rate, but it hurt like hell!

Ship Soup

The morning of June 8 found us off the coast of Utah Beach, prepared to enter France and WW II. Ship upon ship, the staging area was stacked full. Cruisers, destroyers and battleships hammered away at fortified German positions. In an assembly line of destruction, the mighty parade sliced parallel to the shoreline. All barrels banged simultaneously as they threw round after round inland. Anti-aircraft, 20mm, 40mm, 8-inch, 16-inch, even .50-caliber machine guns frantically fired westward. One battleship set broadside, right next to us. She hurled 16-inch shells well beyond the coast. The wake from each blast rocked us severely sideways.

The sky buzzed with Allied aircraft. An enemy fighter occasionally braved the scene, but they didn't last long. British or American planes quickly knocked them down or chased them away.

The initial landing forces had already eliminated the enemy's beachfront cannons and machine-gun nests. Left with little else, the Germans lobbed large rounds from long range. Yet, their shells continued to rain on the beach and nearby waters. Huge explosions of sand and sea surrounded us. Although not D-Day, it was enough to scare the hell out of green troops.

Not only was I frightened, but extremely anxious. In my mind, the transfer of troops from ship to shore was taking way too long. I hated sitting in all that mess, helplessly waiting for our turn.

Stubborn Mines

Even at D+2, the water remained thick with floating mines. The sweepers corralled and controlled them as best they could, but they were vastly outnumbered. When a pair, no longer moored, ambled too close to our vessel, the captain called a rifle unit on deck. Although I'm sure there were more clinical methods of detonating mines, shooting at them was all we had. The air crackled with gunfire and one mine let loose almost immediately, a safe distance away. But, the other proved particularly stubborn. Before long, the men stood ankle deep in spent cartridges. Try as they might, they couldn't get it to blow.

Bullets ricocheted in all directions. The mine steadily crept nearer still. Finally, it detonated! But, we were too close. The blast resonated throughout the craft. Was the hull breached? We didn't abandon ship, so the damage must have been minor. Whatever the extent, it was a matter for captain and crew, not ground-pounders. Our concerns lay inland.

Our Turn

Amid scattered explosions, troop ships and transports continued to consummate their unions. A fixed flow of Americans funneled onto Utah Beach. At long last, our turn arrived.

We poured over the side. Nervous soldiers awkwardly lumbered down cargo nets. No matter how nimble you might be, those things always made you look like a lummox. We packed the transport tight and cruised for shore. A steady stream of water sprayed over our heads. Scared and loaded down with gear, we chattered little and moved even less.

Because our packs would take us straight to the bottom, we first worried about being dumped into deep water. One of our resident non-swimmers remedied the situation by having a heart-to-heart discussion with the transport pilot. Let's just say there may have been some not so veiled threats involved, regarding possible retribution for a bad drop. Whether as a deterrent or motivator, fear often worked wonders. We leapt into less than knee-deep water.

When that door went down, we scrambled out in a hurry. No one knew what to expect and we weren't about to take any chances. Getting off that beach topped everyone's list of objectives. We ran as fast as drenched clothes and oversized field packs would allow. Only blurred bootprints remained in our sandy wake. With our path marked, we got on with the show and passed across the causeways. About to leave Utah Beach behind, I took one last look. What a mess! The whole thing resembled a junkyard, mired in two to ten feet of water. Although the dead and wounded had largely been removed, wreckage was strewn everywhere.

I noticed a significant communication tower, piggybacked on a 2.5-ton truck. The vehicle set deep, submerged to the roof. A bulldozer worked feverishly to free it from the sea. The focal point of much frenzied commotion, that radio equipment surely seemed important. Perhaps it numbered among Ike's master brush strokes—his way to stay apprised of the situation.

Instead of hooking the chains to the truck, the recovery crew clamped them onto the station and tower. When that dozer yanked, it pulled all that precious cargo right into the water. I couldn't help but laugh at another ingenious plan scrapped. But, the hedgerows of Normandy would soon wipe the smile from my face. With Utah Beach behind us, we moved inland.

Chapter 3

My Wake-up Call

Utah Beach to Chef du Pont, France

Initial Shots Fired

Lieutenant Bruno Rakowski headed up my platoon. Sergeant Herbert Roeglin worked directly under him. I felt fortunate to serve with each man. Both were top-of-the-line leaders. As an extra, I filled in where needed.

Broom detail, ready for action - Camp Barkeley, TX. Sergeant Herbert Roeglin far left.

From the beach, we pressed along a roadway to witness our first dead bodies. There was nothing seasoned about us as we took these initial steps into combat. The early glance at mortality shocked us all.

Human carnage lined the lanes of Normandy. Here a German jeep driver met his end by American fire - June 1944.

It wasn't long before we found ourselves in the midst of Normandy's hedgerows. The tangled mess of trees and bushes served as natural fencing for each farmer's two to ten acre field. They grew unimaginably thick and at times, were almost impenetrable. Worst of all, they provided excellent cover for a waiting enemy.

A few hours in, our company commander, Captain Marsh ordered a break to grab a breath, get rid of our water coatings and gain perspective. We took cover in a ditch. Not unlike any other, it sliced between the road and neighboring hedgerow.

U. S. Army Signal Corps Photo, Courtesy National Archives

Ever deeper into the hedgerows of Normandy, the 90th Division passes by a gutted French village - June 1944.

I lay next to Rakowski when he asked, "You going to be able to take all this killing, Sergeant?"

Now that I look back, he was probably trying to feel me out. Did I have what it took? How would I react when things got tough? Yet unaware of the answer, I could only reply, "I guess we'll find out."

So many questions remained unanswered. I hoped and prayed that when the time came, I would possess the courage to be a good soldier and not let these men down.

Our bodies stiffened as we both noticed a slapping sound coming from the other side of the tree line. Rakowski bellied his way to the thicket and peered through. He quickly returned, clearly troubled.

"Go take a look," he mumbled in my direction.

I peaked through the bushes to view a 600-pound sow sloppily rooting through the exposed stomach of a dead German soldier. What a mess! After only a brief glimpse,

I'd seen enough and squirmed back to my former spot without uttering a single word.

"Aren't you going to do something about that?" Rakowski questioned. Square-jawed and strong as an ox, he was built for war. Yet apparently, he possessed little tolerance for farm animals, or at least, that one.

M Company Photo by David Pond Willis

Lieutenant Bruno Rakowski
M Company, 358th Infantry

Again stumped for an answer, I didn't respond. He crawled close to my face and calmly ordered, "Take care of it, Sergeant."

I stuck my head and shoulders back through the hedgerow and emptied my M1 into the dumb beast. Although at a very large French pig instead of an enemy soldier, I was perhaps the first in our unit to fire a round in WW II. Mission accomplished, I returned to the ditch and reloaded.

Our First Night

Initially, we made little progress. That night, we dug in deep. We set up, two men to a foxhole. One napped, while the other stood guard—not that anyone could sleep.

Things settled down. Platoon and section sergeants walked rounds to check on their guys. A short, stocky, extremely likable sergeant from central Texas was doing just that when one of his men mistook him for a Kraut, panicked and pulled the trigger. Wounded badly, the sergeant dropped. Medics worked on him for hours, but he didn't survive. He was our first to die.

Tortured by his own regret, the young private also suffered severely. Within earshot of his foxhole, I listened to this broken man moan and cry all night. War wasn't supposed to be like this. The cheering crowds and holiday parades were long gone, replaced by death and destruction.

The mistakes sometimes hurt the most. You couldn't take them back. You couldn't erase them. Yet, you couldn't live with them either. I'm quite certain a part of the shooter died too that day. None of us slept a wink.

Lesson Learned

The next day brought increasing action. We crossed paths with many American paratroopers from the 82nd and 101st Airborne Divisions — truly a different breed. Some were dead, others wounded, many still fighting on.

I remember one leaning back against a corner hedgerow. He manned a light machine gun. A spattering of spent shell casings surrounded him. Across his field of fire lay ten to twenty rotting German corpses.

The paratrooper was also dead, his body riddled with bullet holes. Up to that point, my knowledge of war read like a blank chalkboard. The unforgettable scene added scratches, scrawled notes. I started to fathom the true meaning of words like "courage" and "bravery." This warrior fired until his last breath, fully aware and accepting of his final fate. He was a small piece of a much larger picture, and knew it. In death, this heroic young American taught me a valuable early lesson on sacrifice. I was only one of many, with a cause greater than each part.

Special Delivery

Down the lane, we hit stiff resistance in a cluster of houses to our left. German snipers and machine gunners packed them full. We attempted to set them ablaze, but struggled mightily. Their fire held ours at bay.

However, we still walked within range of the Navy's big guns. Through spotters, they flattened troublesome targets throughout the region. The fleet off Utah Beach really helped loosen things up inland.

U. S. Army Signal Corps Photo, Courtesy National Archives

90th Division infantrymen clear debris from the streets of a war-torn Normandy village - June 1944.

Huge rounds soon streaked through the sky like falling meteorites. They slammed into our sore spot, the problem structures, with unimaginable force. Unable to contain our emotions, pent-up, boyish enthusiasm spilled over! We cheered raucously, our spirits buoyed by the destructive show! At these initial stages of war, dead enemy soldiers were cause for great celebration. We couldn't act like we'd "been there—done that" because we hadn't. Although we'd trained for years, when it came to real live combat, we were as green as grass in May. By the time the Navy cannons ceased, only rubble remained. Many thanks to our boys in blue!

My First Recon

Throughout the day, the Germans gave sparingly. By dusk, our gains were minimal and again, we dug in. I had just finished my home for the night, when a runner located me with orders to follow him to our command post. Captain Marsh requested my presence.

Frontline headquarters often left a lot to be desired. I found Marsh in a foxhole covered with several raincoats. Under these drapes, he studied maps by the meager light of a small lantern.

"Sergeant Winebrenner, come in," he said, welcoming me into his humble abode. "I have a job for you, Sergeant. Take a small patrol through these woods to Chef du Pont. There, you should find a group of paratroopers. They hold a bridgehead across the Merderet River, west of town. We will be there in the morning. You need to make contact—let them know that we're on our way and to be expecting us."

Captain Marsh had a way about him. When making an important point, he always donned a special look. He raised his right eyebrow in an arch, maybe an inch above the left. When you received the "raised eyebrow," you knew he meant business. I got it that night.

John Marsh was born in Colorado, but moved to Billings, Montana in the 1920s when his father took a position with the Great Western Sugar Company. He graduated from Billings High School in 1933 and attended the University of Montana at Missoula. In the summers, he helped finance his education by driving a tour bus through Yellowstone National Park. In 1938, he graduated with a BA in Business Administration and enrolled at Stanford University in Palo Alto, California. He earned his MBA in 1941 and joined the service shortly thereafter.[1]

M Company Photo by David Pond Willis

Captain John Marsh
M Company, 358th Infantry

From academia to the battlefield, our courageous captain carried many admirable leadership qualities. He was strict, but fair—extremely intelligent, but also personable. He commanded respect without demanding it. Rather than look down his nose at his men, he lifted us up to his level. Without question, he was well-loved and respected, but always in charge. We would follow that man to the ends of the earth. And in the summer of 1944, Normandy wasn't far from it.

Marsh also excelled at map work and strategic positioning. He saw the big picture rather than just the next step. In those early days, our battalion commander, Colonel Bealke often leaned on his ability in this field.

Although I mainly worked in our platoon under Rakowski, whenever Marsh called, I went. He was fully aware of the road I had traveled thus far—knew that I'd grown up in the country, and that I had spent ten weeks at OCS and more than a year at Fort Sill. Like him, I read maps and grasped directions well. Accordingly, he often used me in a reconnaissance capacity.

"Now, when you get close to that village, be very careful," he added in summary. "After what these paratroopers have been through, they'll be firing at just about anything."

With my orders, I returned to camp and gathered my team. At 2:00 a.m., we set out for Chef du Pont. Artificial illumination only occasionally interrupted the moonless night. Near the village, a stray artillery shell sent us digging for cover in a backyard garden. We clicked handheld metal crickets to signal the paratroopers of our friendly nature and we really had those babies singing.

By dawn's early light, we made contact without incident and accomplished our mission. Per Marsh's orders, we then awaited the rest of our unit's arrival.

In a house at the village's edge, we discussed the finer points of war with our newfound friends. One of these paratroopers had cut out the stock of his rifle and pasted in a picture of his girlfriend. To keep her safe and secure, he added a transparent plastic coating. In times of trouble, he rubbed his face on her photograph for good luck.

I privately wondered if it worked. He was still alive—so I guess, so far, so good.

These guys taught me how to cook with plastic explosives. It normally came in two-pound blocks. You just tore off a piece the size of a walnut and lit it with a match. Water boiled for coffee in no time.

Paratroopers, concealed in their foxholes, also manned areas along the bridge. I visited a few to pass the time. While there, I was shocked to see several German soldiers riding down the street on bicycles toward our position. We ducked down and sat in silence. They wheeled closer still. Obviously confused by the blurred front lines, they were unaware of our presence. When they reached a point directly in front of us, two paratroopers with flame-throwers stood up and torched the whole batch.

I can still see the men burning, their tires spinning around on fire. I can still hear their screams in agony. The string of bikes ran into a side ditch and there, the riders burned to death. What a terrible way to go, but it was war.

Afterward, the paratroopers just went back about their business, seemingly unfazed—all in a day's work for this battle-hardened bunch. At this stage, I was still a bit naïve to the whole "war thing." But, this event served as my wake-up call. No more illusions! It was going to get ugly and I'd better prepare myself right now.

By midmorning, our unit arrived. We rejoined them, crossed the Merderet River and continued west toward Picauville—farther inland, deeper into the war.

Chapter 4

Tempers Tried, Friends Lost

Chef du Pont to Picauville, France

Untimely Temper Tantrum
Dense woods and hedgerows dominated the route to Picauville. German artillery pounded our ranks. The dreaded enemy 88s were debilitating at best, deadly at worst. There was nothing more disheartening than fighting an enemy you could not even see. The terror produced by such an anonymous barrage overwhelmed many. Consumed by the stress, minds snapped. Firsthand, we came to know what "shell-shock" and "battle fatigue" looked like, and it wasn't pretty.

The combination of tough terrain and increased enemy fire spread units out. Several smaller and completely separate battles coexisted. Skirmishes between squad-sized outfits replaced massive regimental encounters.

The number of snipers multiplied exponentially. Seemingly in every tree, they often hid under camouflage capes and netting. Some built platforms, closely resembling the hunting stands of today. Yet instead of deer, the riflemen targeted American GIs. Oftentimes, they ran lines from one tree to another. When the front position heated up, they just cabled back to the next. We'd stumbled into a preprogrammed death trap.

In a thickly wooded area, a concealed sniper pinned down a private and me. The marksman fired a Schmeisser submachine gun. I recognized its familiar sound. Like an 88, it sang a distinctive song.

We sought refuge behind a large hump of dirt. He emptied the entire clip each time before pausing to reload, but the bursts always fell a little short. With all the trees, I'm not sure he could see us that well and we had no idea of his location. But, we had to find him, and fast!

"I'm going to move to my left," I told the private. "It'll draw his fire. You see where it comes from!"

Without taking the time to second-guess myself, I rolled to my left, like a barrel down a hill. The rifleman sent another magazine my way, but again missed.

Out of breath, I looked to my partner and panted, "Did you see him?"

My boy lay there, lighting a cigarette. He hadn't even been watching. I got hot, immediately! So angry, I stood up, walked over and proceeded to kick the hell out of him. Of course, that brought even more fire. But at that moment, I didn't care.

"Wake up and open your eyes!" I shouted, then scrambled behind a tree.

The boot massage got his attention. While our assailant threw rounds at my tree and me, the private spotted him. He crawled to the sniper's position and looked up to notice the hobnails shining on the soles of his shoes. With his M1, the young soldier blasted rounds straight up into the tree and took Jerry out. The Kraut was tied in and never fell to the ground, but he was as dead as dirt. The beaming trooper called me over to revel in his success. Still angry, I gave him little credit. Although not quite like I drew it up, the plan worked—no more sniper.

Shortages Of All Kinds

We suffered heavy casualties in this area. Besides the 88 and sniper fire, the German line companies eagerly awaited our arrival. They had dug concealed fortifications into the hedgerows. We unwittingly worked across open pastures, right into their gun barrels. We didn't know their whereabouts until we tasted their steel. But by then, it was too late for many.

U. S. Army Signal Corps Photo, Courtesy National Archives

90th Division infantrymen, accompanied by American armor, work the lanes and hedgerows of Normandy - June 1944.

When caught far from cover, offense was your only defense. If you buried your head or ran backward, enemy gunners picked you off like targets at a tired carnival game. You had to put them on the defensive—force them to fear for their own lives. Our battalion commander, Colonel Bealke, preached it early and often. Although it went against every human instinct, "cover fire and advance forward" was your only way out.

In several spots, the trees and bushes grew so thick that you couldn't get through. Tanks even struggled to pierce these natural barriers. Fully aware of this fact, our enemy laid wait at the gaps between the rows. They baited us to ford these openings into farther fields, but safe passage proved little more than a mirage. After only a short time, piles of dead Americans signaled all latecomers to take roads less traveled.

GI's dropped here, there—everywhere. So many fell that we suffered a shortage of litter carriers. Amid the chaos, I saw Roy Hughes from Doc Bulger's outfit. He, alone in the road, held one end of a stretcher. The other lay on the ground, flanked by a downed bearer. A wounded soldier struggled onboard.

"You need some help, Roy?" I shouted as I leapt up to give him a hand. But then, a huge volley of enemy machine-gun fire sent us both into the ditch. No matter your MOS classification, Normandy was a living nightmare.

To Fight Another Day!

Things backed up at the next hedgerow. Forward progress ground to a halt. Our executive officer, 1st Lieutenant Donald Benedict, not short on guts, crawled ahead with a runner in search of a place to cross.

A graduate of the University of Idaho, Benedict had taught high school vocational-agriculture classes prior to war. As a result of college ROTC, he was a commissioned officer and received his orders following Pearl Harbor.[1] He was intelligent, well-liked among the ranks and certainly a capable second in command to Captain Marsh.

Benedict tested the brush and found a gap. But unbeknownst to him, a concealed enemy sniper tracked his every move. Our XO raised to his knees, ready to advance, but never got the chance. Shots rang out! A round struck Benedict in the face! The bullet penetrated just below the right nostril and exited into his oral cavity. It shattered the roof of his mouth and took seven teeth with it.

M Company Photo by David Pond Willis
1st Lieutenant Donald Benedict
M Company, 358th Infantry

Yet under his own power, Benedict stumbled toward our aid station. In his wake, a trail of blood, saturated bandages, teeth and possibly even the bullet, marked his route.

Along the way, he crossed paths with an old friend. "I didn't realize how bad it was until I witnessed the look on 1st Sergeant Inman's face!" Benedict later admitted. "His expression scared me! With all the blood from my mouth,

I must have really looked a mess!"[2]

Benedict was stabilized and evacuated to England. Amazingly, he survived a gunshot wound to the face to fight another day.

Rallying Cry!

Crouched in a ditch between a lane and a hedgerow, I watched German artillery and mortar shells smash the open road. Deadly accurate, they dealt unspeakable damage.

We couldn't stay there! Hunkering down was the natural reaction and it felt so right, but it was dead wrong! If we allowed them, the enemy would gladly cut us apart with mortar rounds and artillery fire, by the hour, by the day. They wouldn't even have to get their hands dirty.

Rather than die in place, I crept up the line. Forward was our only alternative. The horrible cries I heard along the way haunt me yet today. The terrified and dying alike begged for mercy from God and mother. Most men moved out of my way, but one young private wouldn't budge. I slapped him on the shoulder to let him know I was there and coming through, but still got no response. He shivered uncontrollably—his eyes empty and mind gone. With the air full of flying metal fragments, I didn't really want to leave the cover of that ditch. So, I began to lumber over his body. That's when I noticed that he couldn't move. His legs were gone, shredded by an enemy mortar shell. Just a boy, he calmly waited for death as screams for "Medic!" permeated the chaos.

With each additional barrage, more and more of the enemy artillery rounds released a colored smoke, instead of exploding on impact. This fueled an even greater concern, almost a panic, along our lines. Gas masks were gone, discarded long ago. We all thought of them as more of an encumbrance than an essential item. That is, until that moment.

Like fire on a fuse, the word spread down our ranks, "The Germans are gassing us!"

Fragile psyches began to fold! Our line wavered! All appeared lost, when up the lane strode big old rough, tough Colonel Thompson, the 358th Regimental Commander.

He used a carbine as a walking stick. His size made it look small. Slowly he sauntered up and down the road, impervious to the incoming rounds.

"Guess we're going to have to slow these boys down before this whole thing caves in!" he thought aloud.

I didn't say a word. My mind was still processing fallen friends, exploding shells and the possibility of gas. He fully absorbed the scene before pacing forty feet up the lane, near the middle of our faltering ranks.

"All right! Soldiers stop where you are!" he bellowed. "Turn around and head back to your positions! We must press on! We must fight!" No one desired a duel with Thompson.

In support, from the ditch down the lane, rose a courageous Californian. Open and amiable, he was a friend of mine who never missed an opportunity to show me pictures of his family and girlfriend back home. Handsome too, he grew loads of wavy red hair atop his head.

He worked the lines, pumped his fist and rallied the troops. But in the blink of an eye, a German mortar round landed at his feet. He never knew what hit him. The blast literally blew him apart as bits of smoldering flesh littered the lane. I stared in shock, then whirled away.

I never got used to the rapid rate of war—the absolute immediacy of the killing. Men were gone in no more time than it took to flip a light switch from on to off—life to death. Yet, their absences would be felt for decades, if not centuries.

The words and actions of these two stopped the retreat. Men fell back into place and once again toed the line. The shells releasing the colored smoke turned out to be marker rounds. Captured Eastern Europeans, forced into service, manned many German gun crews. Whenever possible, they purposely slipped in duds to hinder the enemy effort.

Shortly after the visit, Colonel Thompson himself was pinned down and severely wounded. What a jumbled mess! There were as many Germans behind us as in front of us.

Hobert Winebrenner returns to Normandy,
pictured at the 90th Division Memorial, Utah Beach.

I returned to Normandy in 1970 and among other things, searched for this very road that had seen so much. After hours of trekking down every country lane between Chef du Pont and Picauville, I finally found it. The trees had grown in density. They not only flanked both roadsides, but also connected overtop. The tangle formed a deep, dark and damp tunnel—appropriate considering what had happened there. After twenty-five years, I thought I'd be able to handle it, but I was wrong. The memories were still too vivid, the fragrances too fresh. I stayed for only a moment, then vowed never to return. Some things are better left alone.

"My Section Was Gone!"

We continued to fight and gained any ground we could afford. Bloodied badly, we eventually shoved our way beyond an apple orchard, to the next hedgerow. Per usual, Lieutenant Rakowski blazed the trail. He always led by example and never asked anything of his men that he himself would not do.

Pastures and forests again separated our greater unit. We were spread thin. Our small group manned at least one heavy machine gun, accompanied by small arms support, but Rakowski wanted more.

"Sergeant Winebrenner, we've got good ground here!" he heatedly announced. "But we're outgunned! We need more firepower! Find some fast!"

With my orders, I started back for help. The first person I met was Amon Hartwick, my old friend from Fort Sill. He was a section sergeant in "M" and a good one at that. I explained the situation and he went right to work.

Hartwick pushed his men and machine guns to the front. He first conferred with Rakowski and then barked orders down the line. His crew, maybe two dozen strong, quickly pulled off the arrangement, ready to roll. But at show time, nothing happened! Neither machine gun fire nor spent shell casings sliced through the air, only silence. Their guns jammed!

It had been one extremely hectic day that left little time for proper gun maintenance. Whether the receivers were dry of oil or fouled with dirt, Hartwick's heavy machine guns just wouldn't work. If Rakowski wasn't juiced enough already, he was now livid.

Hartwick stuck by his men. He gathered his section and moved them back to the apple orchard, where they desperately worked to free up their guns. His squad fully intended to return to the fray, but it wasn't meant to be. An enemy artillery spotter watched them exit the field and called in a strike. Multiple 88 shells soon decimated the area. Without foxholes or cover of any kind, the group had no chance.

"My section was gone!" Hartwick later mourned. "I only remember one of my guys not killed or wounded. ...I looked down at my gunner, Guy Wooderson. He'd been hit so bad in the head that all I could see were his brains."[3]

Those who knew Guy will never forget him. Although he hailed from sparsely populated, rural Grant County, Oklahoma, he was the free spirit of our gang, with personality to spare. Right before we shipped out from New York City, he met and married a girl, all in a matter of weeks. But now, he was dead, and she, a widow. Today, Guy's remains rest peacefully at Spring Creek Cemetery, not far from his boyhood home.[4]

Hartwick himself also suffered extensive wounds. Heavy shrapnel cut into his face, mouth and jaw. A large piece struck his arm with such force that it severed his ulna, knocking a chunk of the bone loose. Just days in, his war was over.[5]

As evening approached, we had yet to cover the short distance from Chef du Pont to Picauville. Except for casualties, we showed little for our day's work. With Benedict, Hartwick, Wooderson and many others gone, we stood well understrength. Bad spiraled to worse when word soon circulated of massive enemy numbers, including tanks, forming on the horizon.[6] Outgunned and outmanned, we braced for nightfall.

Private Guy Wooderson
M Company, 358th Infantry
KIA – June 12, 1944 Picauville, France

Chapter 5

We're All In God's Hands

Picauville to Pont l' Abbe, France

Through The Night

Captain Marsh assembled our defenses, a perimeter box. He placed heavy machine guns in each corner of the square and overlapped their fields of fire. Riflemen spanned the reaches between. Our mortar platoon settled in the middle, able to turn in any direction. Packed tight, there were no gaps. Marsh never took his responsibility lightly. When it came to the lives of his men, he was all business—serious and disciplined.

We readied our weaponry, then dug in deep. The Air Corps arrived to lend a hand. A C-47 circled our position and dropped long lasting flares to illuminate the scene. Although far from daylight, it was the next best thing and aided our efforts tremendously.

Many of us privately pondered if we'd live to see the sunrise as night came east of Picauville. The Krauts countered with artillery, mortars and then, men. Gun barrels smoked and shimmered in the darkness, searing hot. I manned an open BAR and just kept firing at anything attempting to bust through the box.

Although I'm not proud of it, killing came with the territory. After all, they were shooting at me! They were trying to kill me! It was either them or me! At that moment, the choice wasn't difficult. You didn't have time to contemplate larger matters of the human race or philosophies of war. You acted on instinct, identified targets, aimed and fired.

I'd grown to hate the German Army. No longer some obscure, far-off presence, they'd touched me personally. In their quest for world domination, they'd killed and maimed buddies all around me. Under those circumstances, hate, the most visceral of emotions, came quite naturally.

Ammo Anyone?

We held tight throughout the night. Thankfully, the intelligence reports concerning enemy armor turned out to be flawed. We saw no tanks. Yet, as the horizon hinted at morning with a dull glow, we found ourselves almost entirely out of ammunition. Rationing ammo was the earmark of a desperate bunch whose time was short. We wore it well.

Just as we feared all might be lost, Gail Hohman arrived with a fresh supply. As transportation corporal, he headed our small motor pool, which consisted of about a dozen jeeps and half-ton trailers for each. Whenever we ran low on anything from batteries to water to ammunition, he made things happen.

Gail rambled through our rear lines shortly before daybreak. He'd convinced a couple of tankers to help us out. They led the way. He followed with two or three of our jeeps and their trailers, stacked tall with ammunition. The new day finally dawned. We had survived!

Corporal Gail Hohman
M Company, 358th Infantry

Too Close For Comfort

Unable to crack our defenses, the Germans backed off at sunrise. We rolled west toward Pont l' Abbe. While en route, we began to hear a distant murmur. In seconds, the sound pitched to a roar, high overhead.

1st Sergeant Inman looked at me and yelled above the noise, "Here we go, Wino! Stukas!"

We all stopped and stared anxiously upward. I recognized their familiar shape and bellowed back, "Not this time, Sergeant; those are our boys!"

A dozen planes packed the small formation. Curiosity turned to panic when we witnessed the black specs fall from their bellies. Everyone ran for his life! Luckily, our retreating enemy had left a ready supply of foxholes. Guys darted every which way, popped below the surface and hid inside their helmets. Inman and I fled into the same small field to find cover in the nick of time.

The concussion shook the earth with unimaginable force. I peered over the edge of my hole to watch leaves and grass suspended in air, not for an instant, but for what seemed like an eternity. Dirt flew in all directions! Although fresh with combat experience, I'd never been bombed. I wouldn't forget it!

As quickly as they filled the morning sky, the bombers vanished. It took us considerable time to shake the shock from our systems. Officers labored long and hard to get their men back under control. We never found out how or why it happened, but instead, just got on with life.

Cider, On The House

Artillery and the Air Corps prepped our next objective, Pont I' Abbe. Outside the village, Captain Marsh again rang my number. He ordered me to gather a recon squad to see what was left in town.

Just like at the schoolyard, I picked a team, and we headed out. Into the burg's east side, we met a group of stragglers almost immediately. "Mit kommen zie, die hande hoch!" I yelled in my best, but terribly broken German. I meant to say, "Come with your hands up!" In an act of surrender, they fanned white undershirts above their heads. So whatever I actually barked hit close enough to home for them to understand.

We herded them into a building at the corner of a crossroads intersection. We definitely picked the right place! Inside set two 500-gallon wooden kegs full of cider, no doubt for making calvados. A thirsty bunch in desperate need of a good stiff drink, we pierced the barrels and helped ourselves. The cider streamed out, like from a fountain, and was pretty strong stuff.

While the guys chatted, I returned to the street. From my west, I heard a breach block slam shut. Recognizing what the sound meant, I raced for cover. An 88 shell screamed over my position and smashed into a house toward Picauville.

In only the last few days, I had learned that as soon as the breach block closed on an 88, it fired. Keenly aware of this fact, I cautiously stepped back into the lane for another look. As recon, I wanted to see the weapon, just to make sure that it wasn't a tank. On cue, the block again smacked shut. I hit the dirt as the second shell dismantled a concrete post 200 feet down the road. I'd seen enough. The shots originated from a mobile artillery piece, pulled by a horse team. Going instead of coming, it ceased fire when I stopped making myself visible.

Why Him And Not Me?

We noticed several vacant foxholes and abandoned fighting positions. The town was small and appeared empty. Apart from our shell-shocked prisoners, we had yet to encounter a live German.

Across from our cider building sat a large stone structure. It looked like a church, but I believe it was a private residence. The enormous crucifix in front caught everyone's eye. It towered as tall as the rooftop. With seemingly little cause for concern, I climbed the five or six steps to the cross's elevated level. I tried to read the plaque at its base, but couldn't because the inscription was in French. Another from my team wandered over and I trotted down to meet him. We spoke for a moment about nothing in particular before he similarly ascended to the cross.

After giving it a casual glance, he turned to me and asked, "Hey Sergeant, what does this say?"

As the words left his mouth, a single shot rang out. The round ripped through the center of his chest, from the back out the front. The bullet's momentum pushed him into a tumble down the steps. His body came to a rest at my feet. Stunned, I grabbed him by the ankles and dragged his lifeless frame across the lane to our hangout. Once inside, I stood stiff, my mind in shock. Someone checked him out, but the gaping chest wound told the story. He was dead before hitting the ground.

My squad had heard the blast and was already scanning the horizon. We located the enemy rifleman in a tree to the rear of the cross. In an attempt to even the score, we sent that Jerry marksman everything we had. The entire middle section of the tree, including branches, leaves and sniper, disintegrated in a hailstorm of steel. Although it felt right to kill this man, it didn't bring back our friend.

New to recon, I learned the ropes the hard way. It hurt unimaginably to lose a man. I felt responsible for his death. I made mistakes, but tried hard never to repeat them. The price was too damn steep.

And why him and not me? There, only minutes before him, why wasn't it me that was shot at the top of the steps? Why am I alive today and he's been dead for sixty years? More than ever, I realized that we were all in God's hands, to come and go as He saw fit.

After announcing our position, we caught some token fire from the west. Although the resistance felt light, there were definitely Germans in town. That was enough for me. We gathered our POWs, one GI - KIA and rejoined our unit outside the village.

The cost of recon often exceeded the benefit. Our outfit never even entered Pont l' Abbe, but instead, chose an alternate course. We dug in north of town.

Hobert and Marian Winebrenner sit at the base of the Pont l' Abbe cross, 1970. Some memories don't fade.

Ammo Run

The next morning, we stormed enemy positions west of Pont l' Abbe. The going was extremely difficult, but we made steady progress. With each new sunrise, the killing only increased.

At one point during the very long day, we ran dangerously low on ammo. Again as an extra sergeant, on orders from Rakowski, I worked my way to the rear, in search of more.

I hoped to find our supply trailers. Not only did they haul machine gun ammunition, but also mortar rounds. For this reason, they most often shadowed our mortar platoon, toward the rear. I recognized the sound of our 81mm tubes better than my own mother's voice and ran in that direction.

For speed's sake, I cut across an open three-to four-acre field. Enemy mortar shells boomed all around me. The explosions knocked me to the ground, where I cowered momentarily. It's not that I'd been zeroed in; the air was just that thick with random fire. Another round landed even closer, but thankfully refused to detonate. Parallel to the dud, my eyes locked on its tail fin protruding from the mud—a stunning reminder of what should have been. If not before, I now regretted my route.

Almost panicked, I leapt to my feet and resumed my sprint across the pasture. Even at full speed, it all seemed like slow motion. Through a few more fields, I finally stumbled on one of our drivers, Henry Rezac. He led me to an entire trailer full of the good stuff. Two people could handle twice as much, so I invited him to tag along. He agreed to join me, although less than enthusiastically.

Our eyes were far larger than our muscles. We loaded up with more boxes and belts of machine-gun ammunition than any two men could rightly carry. The effort could have been measured on the horsepower scale. I don't know what we were thinking. "More is better" obviously dominated our rationale, but it was way too much.

We hung the majority of the ammo over our shoulders and carried the remainder in our arms. By a few hundred yards into the journey, we were both physically exhausted. Yet, we continued.

In need of a breather, we fell on our faces just inside the entryway to a heavily shelled farmhouse. Rezac noticed a commotion in one of the back rooms and loosened his load to investigate. I didn't bother. Instead, I panted like a dog in the summer heat, sucked in air with my mouth wide open.

Henry Rezac
M Company, 358th Infantry

The sound of pistol shots soon roused me from my trance. I raced to the rear to find Rezac standing over a dead German soldier. Everywhere we went, the enemy seemed to be waiting. Apparently quicker on the draw, Henry had won the confrontation.

"I couldn't help it," he lamented. "The guy went for his rifle!" Rezac didn't have to apologize to me.

After several more brief respites, we arrived and collapsed at our final destination. Others noticed our presence and hurried a team over to finish our work. Once up, Henry headed back to his jeeps and job.

That night, we backed off to positions north of Pont l' Abbe and again, dug in. I didn't know how much more I could take. I was physically and mentally spent.

Chapter 6

A Day And Night To Remember

Pont l' Abbe to Gourbesville, France

Relieved?

At about 1:00 a.m., a runner approached with news from headquarters. The 9th Infantry Division was relieving us. We gladly guided them into our bootprints, then filtered back through the lines to a staging area at the rear.

I didn't know it then, but my old Camp Wolters buddy, Bob Smith, with his "Marion" tattoo, served with that group. Small world, huh? They had seen tough action throughout North Africa and were now trying on Europe for size.

We removed from the field to find trucks awaiting our arrival. Up until that point, we had traveled only on foot. Wouldn't it be nice to take a leisurely drive through the French countryside?

Moreover, we believed the term "relieved" to mean we

were destined for someplace cushy, maybe a nice warm spot in the sun. They certainly wouldn't pluck us from one hell on earth, just to drop us into another. Or, would they?

The ride was a short one. We trucked five to ten miles north and unloaded outside of Gourbesville, France. Among nondescript hedgerows, we began to scratch at the soil, some more seriously than others. I'd already excavated one hole north of Pont I' Abbe. Well into my second, I felt as if I'd been burrowing all night long. It wasn't far from the truth.

Everyone was worn-out! I'm not sure any of us had slept much, if at all, since our landing. The hours and days blended into a blurred continuum. Our tanks ran on empty, juiced only by adrenaline.

A Premonition

A sinking feeling from within, perhaps despair fueled by exhaustion, consumed me that morning. I experienced a strong premonition that I wouldn't survive the day. My gut told me, I'd be dead by sundown.

I believed in God, but never put much stock into seeing or feeling the future. A little embarrassed, I longed to keep the thoughts to myself, but they were too strong. I shared them with a select few.

Lieutenant Rakowski caught wind of my vision and attempted to chase it from my head. Try as he might, it remained. I felt as if I'd already read the last chapter to the story of my life. It was time to live it.

It Began With A Bang!

Trucked into the area only hours earlier, we had no time to recon a stone's throw, let alone our greater surroundings. We knew nothing about that piece of dirt or the force we faced. Half dug in along a hedgerow, we lay in wait, ready to advance.

Yet, there was no need for travel. Jerry paid us the rudest of house calls. The Krauts zeroed in our line and specifically targeted a gun emplacement or two. Beyond accurate, their barrage was dead on! Enemy mortar rounds and 88 shells smashed my immediate area like a hammer on a nail!

I was speaking with another soldier, I think it was Sergeant Dean Warren, when the enemy rain began to fall. Although out of my foxhole, I was luckily lying on my front, in a prone position, when a shell exploded overhead. The same red-hot shrapnel hit both of us. He was kneeling beside me at the time of the attack. I rolled on my backside to see his shirt soaked blood red. I sat up from the waist and screamed "Medic! Help! Medic!" over and again.

One arrived in short order. Doc Bulger's boy patched the other soldier up, then litter carriers moved him out.

"Let's have a look at you, Sergeant!" the aidman then said to me.

Confused, I didn't speak. I hadn't even thought about myself being wounded.

"We'd better get you bandaged up!" he continued. "You're leaking a lot of blood!"

That was the first I realized that I'd been hit, too. As my brain registered the injuries, my body felt the pain. On my stomach at the time of the incident, I suffered multiple shrapnel wounds along my backside. Although fragments broke the skin in several spots, two in particular stood out. A large piece of metal had entered my left leg and cut to the bone. Another sliced particularly deep above my buttocks, near the base of my spine. Yet, I was alive.

More Than Me

My plight was far from unique. Casualties cluttered the local landscape. Only minutes before the pounding, I had spoken with Sergeant Oliver Rogers about our machine gun ammo, or lack thereof. A tough, young East Texan from Harrison County, he was gone just that quick, killed instantly.

M Company Photo by David Pond Willis
Sergeant Oliver Rogers
M Company, 358th Infantry
KIA – June 15, 1944 Gourbesville, France

The same burst that hit Rogers also tore into one of his men, machine gunner, Allan McInnis. While still at Camp Barkeley, our less than silent southern majority had affectionately dubbed McInnis our "blue belly" because of his Yankee roots. He hailed from Saco, Maine.

Wounded, wrapped and on his way to England, McInnis committed his dead friend's final thoughts to memory, never to be forgotten. "Sergeant Rogers wasn't an outwardly religious man, but he spoke of God that morning," McInnis later admitted. "Sure, he could be a little rough around the edges, but he was no atheist either.

There were no atheists in foxholes. Right before the attack, he mentioned to me, 'It sure looks like the good Lord took care of us last night!' Then it hit! Those were his last words."[1] The earthly remains of Platoon Sergeant Oliver Z. Rogers rest peacefully in Harrison County, Texas's Gum Springs Cemetery, near his old stomping grounds.[2]

Although I wasn't aware of it at the time, and wouldn't find out until months later, one of my best friends, Sergeant Ray Krolick died, too, that day. A big Polish lug from St. Louis, he could rattle his teeth in such a way that sounded like shaking dice. Given such an advantage, he always won big at the crapshoots.

M Company Photo by David Pond Willis

Sergeant Ray Krolick
M Company, 358th Infantry
KIA – June 15, 1944 Gourbesville, France

Strong as an ox, he could carry four ammo cans by the hour and never say a word about it. When we'd head into battle, he'd always pop his head up and yell toward me, "What's the word, Wino?"

And I'd return, "Let's give 'em hell!" He'd grin, rattle those teeth and away we'd go.

Underneath the tough exterior, Ray had a heart of gold. He'd do anything for you, including lay down his life. As an American soldier, he gave full measure.

So Begins Another Journey

Once bandaged, I struggled to my feet. My medic stared suspiciously, then advised, "You better hang here for a litter team!" He then packed his gear and raced to answer one of the other many remaining cries for help. I paused for a time, but there were no litter carriers around. Again, our casualties far exceeded the number of those assigned to care for them. Rather than wait who knows how long for the next available ride, I chose to go it alone. Patience was not one of my strong suits. Although a little wobbly, I could walk. Being somewhat functional, I just assumed that I could locate our aid station on my own. After all, how hard could it be?

I began this trek by throwing down my weapon, an M1. I don't know why. Maybe I thought I was heading back into relative safety or that my war was over. Either way, I was badly mistaken.

The big picture eluded me. Today, if given the chance to describe Normandy in one phrase, I'd shout, "Violent mass confusion!" But back then, I never fully grasped the extent of the chaos surrounding me. Lines lay disconnected and flanks, wide open. The Germans not only fought in front of us, but also in back. Opposing pockets waged tiny wars all over the battlefield—all over the peninsula. No one, anywhere, was truly safe.

Even more than that, I wasn't in anyway familiar with

the area. I had walked from Utah Beach to Pont l' Abbe and knew that route well. But trucked into Gourbesville only the night before, I didn't have a clue. The fields and roads all looked alike to me.

I staggered back and left, in what I believed to be the direction to our makeshift medical facilities. I first crawled through a hedgerow into an open field. I hugged the tree line, but still caught some random fire.

I soon happened on a row of fallen Americans. No doubt caught by surprise in a skirmish line, their corpses lay head to toe. I now thought better of my earlier action and picked up one of their rifles. They didn't need it anymore.

I labored to maintain bearings and balance alike. My head felt foggy. I leaned on a gate for a moment's rest. On the other side ran a small sunken lane. Beyond it and to my left, I noticed a battered French farmhouse. Directly across from me was a tiny barn with a huge tree in back.

While I climbed over the locked gate, a wide-shoul-dered GI popped out of the ditch. A 1st sergeant from another regiment, he suffered from an arm wound. We'd seen each other before, but had never spoken.

As he and I conversed, two other walking wounded joined our group, a T/5 corporal and a private. I didn't notice the corporal's injuries. But like the sergeant, the private had a bum arm. We were now a collection of four.

"Where you headed?" the 1st sergeant asked me.

"Left, down this lane," I answered. "I think it's the way to our aid station."

He adamantly disagreed and we argued for a short time. Eventually, he pulled rank. "We're going this way together and that's it!" he ordered.

We gathered in a "V" formation and headed to our right. The 1st sergeant and corporal led the way, just a few feet apart. The private and I followed, fanned out slightly on the flanks. We maintained a sizable gap, maybe twenty yards, between them and us.

The road took a sharp turn to the left about a mile down. As we approached this bend, the air popped with machine-gun fire. Completely concealed and unbeknownst to us, a German gun crew had built a nest in the corner.

The bullets ripped through our two in the lead. I saw their shirts puff out and then tear as the shells exited their backsides. The intense fire kept them afloat for a time. When they finally fell, both were already dead.

I scrambled into the ditch. Surely, the next volley had my name on it. The private raced back down the middle of the lane. But amazingly, he didn't attract any fire! I was shocked that they weren't shooting at him! Then I thought, "Maybe their gun's jammed."

That ditch certainly offered no solutions. Sooner or later, they'd get me. I rose to my feet and hobbled after him. I pulled with my good leg and dragged my wounded one behind, just as fast as I could go. Once more, they didn't fire! It's another of those things that I'll never fully comprehend.

I tried to keep pace with the private, but he was too damn fast and left me far behind. By the time I reached the gate, I was again physically exhausted. My saturated bandages no longer stemmed the flow of blood. My pants were soaked and my left boot, filled. It squished loudly with each additional step. I limped around behind the barn and sat with my back against the big tree. Between gasps for air, I attempted to collect myself. Oh, how I wished I had waited on those litter carriers!

My Life Spared

I began to hear Germans talking in the distance. Their voices steadily increased in volume. I correctly assumed they were searching for me.

Thigh-high grass provided some cover, but would it be enough? I crouched low to the ground and tried to hide. "Maybe they won't see me," I privately hoped. But their sounds became louder still and they closed in.

I quietly removed the clip from the carbine I'd taken off the dead American. Down to my last chance, I retrieved the oiler from the stock. I wanted to make sure that thing worked, but the oiler was empty.

With no other choice, I silently shucked the shells from the clip, one by one. Only five remained. I grasped each separately between my fingers and rubbed it through my greasy locks. After several days of sweating profusely, my hair held natural lubricant to spare. I returned four to the clip and put one in the chamber.

The enemy squad beat the bushes and continued along the lane. I visually made out at least eight of them. With only five shells, I understood this wasn't going to end well. There alone, I accepted my fate. If and when they discovered me, I thought I might get three real quick and then let the cards fall where they would.

I raised my carbine and took aim. They still hadn't spotted me. I sighted in the first, but felt a strange sensation, like being watched. Before pulling the trigger, I turned toward the barn. Not more than ten feet away, a Kraut sergeant leveled his weapon at my head. He had me! While the others had noisily lumbered along the hedgerow, he had quietly stalked behind the barn. Occupied with them, I didn't see or hear him at all.

With an enemy weapon to my head while mine pointed in another direction, I knew my jig was up. I carefully laid my rifle on the ground in front of me and put my hands on top of my head. I was a POW.

He calmly walked over, kicked my gun away and then called his crew. I could tell he was in charge, something like a section sergeant. The others all seemed younger and less in control. One fresh face, surely no older than a teenager, strongly desired to kill me outright. For a greeting, he mockingly slapped my face, then booted me hard several times in the chest and stomach. I reeled in pain, doubled over and sucked for air. Thankfully, the sergeant stepped in to push him aside.

Others approached with my former companion, the wounded private. His health had slipped considerably. Whether they shot or beat him within an inch of his life, I don't know. But, he now knocked at death's door.

We prepared to move out, but the young enemy soldier had to have one last go at me. This time, he clubbed me in the face with the butt of his rifle. The blow turned me out like a light. Most of the damage was done around my right eye and socket. Of all my wartime injuries, this wound gives me the most trouble today. Since that beating, it has never been right.

I awoke sometime later in a different setting with the private sprawled out beside me. Our captors fought from a nearby hedgerow. They must have just dragged us along and dropped us in the middle of this field. We lay unguarded, but still within their sights—still POWs.

They battled for their own lives and definitely had their hands full. Several slumped behind the row, either dead or severely wounded. At that instant, we were the last things on their minds.

Two Becomes One

My companion eventually succumbed to his wounds. He died by my side in the middle of that anonymous field, somewhere in Normandy. Able to do little else, I closed his eyes. I'm sorry to say that I never knew his name. Two became one as I was again, alone.

From the combination of no sleep, excessive loss of blood and a rifle butt to the face, I drifted in and out of consciousness. In one of my more lucid moments, I again recognized the echo of our 81mm mortars.

Evening approached and I realized this might be my last opportunity for escape—for life in general. The grass stood tall, maybe a couple of feet high. I used it and the impending darkness for cover. I began to crawl toward the familiar sounds of our launching tubes.

My captors still swapped shells with their American counterparts and thankfully remained preoccupied. I slowly sidled away, a few feet at a time. I inched farther and farther until I came to the opposite hedgerow, where I poured myself through. I dropped several feet into a deep, sunken side ditch and once more, lost consciousness—out cold, but free at last!

The Cold Arms Of Death

Boom! An explosion woke me from my stupor. A medical team from one of our sister regiments had driven their jeep down the lane, past my position and hit a land mine. The men in front, a driver and a captain lay dead. The two medics riding in the rear survived and were helping each other back to their aid station. What time? What day? I had no clue.

Deep into the night, the moonlight and a nearby house fire illuminated the scene. In coming to, I finally took note of my surroundings. I rested in a ditch full of dead Krauts and American GIs. Several corpses, cold and stiff nudged against my frame. Rigid arms draped over me with dead eyes wide open. The whole mix scared me beyond belief! I panicked, flailed about like a drowning child and screamed, "Help! Help me! Help!"

My ghastly shriek almost sent the two aidmen into cardiac arrest. They could see that dead soldiers filled the ditch, but having one come to life was not what they were expecting. They eventually pulled me out and sandwiched me between them. Each supported one of my arms. Three wounded men limped along in the darkness.

It seemed like we stumbled on forever, but they knew

the way. We finally arrived at an old farmhouse and moved to the side entrance. It was their aid station. Blankets covered the doors and windows to black out the glow from inside lamps. We stepped into the kitchen. Coal-oil lanterns provided limited lighting. Busy arms grabbed me before I hit the floor. My earthly fate fell into their hands.

Field Hospital ER

At first, they laid me on the kitchen table like a slab of meat. The attending medic located only a faint pulse.

"We have to get some plasma in this guy, now!" he spoke in earnest.

While he worked on my arm, another cut off my left boot and pant leg. Some cleaned and bandaged, while others still struggled to start a line.

"This guy's lost so much blood all his veins have collapsed," one announced. "They're so flat, I can't get a needle in!" On hearing that, I again lost consciousness for a time.

When I awoke, I was now lying on a stretcher. I heard a new voice in the room and sensed his urgency.

"Get the stretcher up on the table and lift the end with his feet higher than his head!" the man barked.

They elevated my feet and the entire room slid off the edge of my world. Everything spun. I could not right my ship. I questioned over and over again, "Where am I? What's going on?" Although I reached mightily, I just couldn't grasp the reality of it all.

"I'm in!" exclaimed one of the team. He successfully started a line.

The plasma surged throughout my deprived system. I felt stronger almost immediately. In time, the fog enveloping my head finally began to lift. Through this medical team's heroic efforts and by the grace of God, I found myself back in the land of the living, or at least, land of the semi-coherent.

Back To The Beach

They covered me well and set my stretcher in the corner of the room. I heard a jeep drive up and stop outside the door. The men carefully placed me onto the back, along with one other. Off we sped. My body hurt more with each bump in the road.

We arrived at a huge tent. I could hear the ocean in the background, with the waves washing ashore. It sounded so peaceful, a far cry from the savagery just a few miles inland. Wounded GIs packed the tent full. They laid me on a table, beneath a very bright light. After removing my bandages, they took a better look at the wounds on my back, legs, thigh, rear and eye.

This was apparently an assessment or evaluation station. The officer in charge quickly concluded, "Let them take care of this one back in England."

With my ticket punched, out the end of the tent I went and onto the beach. I raised my head to witness row after row of stretchers. They spanned the sand as far as my eyes could see. There must have been miles of them.

A nurse soon came over to check on me. "Can I get you anything?" she asked. "A drink or something to eat?"

My answer was concise, but complete. "Yes!" I gasped.

This most wonderful woman brought me a tin pie pan full of fruit cocktail. I never looked for a fork or spoon, but instead, just creased the pan in the middle and poured its contents down my throat. It was the best meal I ever had.

Not long after, crews slid us into small transports, maybe a dozen stretchers per boat. They shuttled us out to the LSTs, which waited in deeper water. These "Landing Ship, Tanks" transported armor, artillery and other heavy equipment over from England. Once empty, they raised the flag to become hospital ships, then reloaded with wounded soldiers for the return voyage. They wasted not an inch and stacked us tight like cigarettes in a pack. Once topped-off to the rafters, our vessel headed for England.

Looking Back

In reality, what felt like a lifetime, had only been a few days. Within my one week of war, I had slept and eaten little, if any. I experienced enough carnage to last an eternity. Friends died unimaginable deaths before my very eyes. I had taken human life, while being spared my own. Perhaps most poignant was a German sergeant, who in protecting me from his own men, allowed me to live—saved my life. I didn't know his name, but would never forget his actions.

Yet, I was not alone. Most within my outfit would leave the battlefield in one of two ways, either by stretcher or body bag. Over the last eight days, the 358th Regiment suffered 200 men killed and 806 wounded, almost a full third of our Utah Beach landing force.[3] In Normandy's hedgerows, it wasn't a matter of "if" you'd get hit, but rather "when" and "would you survive." I now realize that as bad as I had it, I was one of the fortunate ones. I lived to fight another day.

Chapter 7

A Time To Heal

Birmingham, England

Back Across The Channel

The harrowing tales proved the best part of our return voyage. Fresh and raw, they were history by only a few hours. The paratroopers wove the most colorful yarns. Firsthand accounts of bad drops behind enemy lines peppered the conversations.

On arrival at Plymouth, England, a dock crane lowered large pallets into our boat. The transport crew quickly filled each with stretchers, maybe a dozen to a skid. The hoist then lifted us up, out, over and into a railway staging area where teams shuffled us onto awaiting hospital trains.

English nurses staffed these cars and treated us like heroes. They even offered us some warmed-up U.S. Army rations. After several connections, we hit the open road and soon rolled into Birmingham, England.

My New Home

Once through the city, we stopped at a vast hospital complex. The strings of Quonset huts, all intertwined, formed one huge grid pattern. From above, it must have resembled an enormous spider web.

Dedicated wards for different wounds ran off the main line. They assigned me to one servicing everything from burns to amputations. I apparently fit somewhere in between. Before I could even settle into bed, they pushed me through X-ray.

A doctor hastily examined my pictures and concluded, "Son, we'll operate on you tomorrow."

"Fine," I thought, not feeling strongly either way.

The next morning, an attendant chauffeured me into an adjacent wing. I assumed it to be the surgery unit, but was mistaken. My driver instead deposited my wheelchair and me in front of yet another doctor. War had washed this man clean of all emotion. Deadpan best described his bedside manner.

"Things have changed for you, Sergeant," he spoke squarely. "Your MOS (Military Occupational Specialty) classification is hot. They need you back at the front. This being the case, we've decided that an operation is not warranted at this time." With that said, he simply walked away.

"OK," I again resolved. I wasn't anything close to a doctor. Confident that this group's collective medical knowledge far exceeded my own, I willingly resigned my care to their hands.

Over the next several weeks, rotating teams of doctors and nurses picked and cleaned my wounds. Shards of shrapnel continued to work their way to the surface. The human body's ability to detect and eject foreign elements astounded me. I'm still amazed by its self-mending qualities. Steadily, I clotted, scabbed and healed.

In an effort to further speed my recovery, they pumped

me full of penicillin—huge doses of the stuff. It was new at the time. But again, I left the doctoring to them. Over the years, I've often wondered if they really knew what they were doing. Or, were we little more than guinea pigs?

Hospital Friendships

My heart sank at seeing so many severely maimed and wounded. The man in the bed next to mine hailed from western Illinois. He'd lost his right eye in battle, but that was only the beginning. Surgeons had recently amputated an arm and a leg. A pulley system tugged at his skin to stretch it over the stumps. He could do little more than look on helplessly.

I found the entire scene terribly depressing. In war, your mind never had the chance to dwell too deeply. But in that hospital, all you had was time. Even though it meant a quicker return to the front, I worked hard at healing.

Soon freed from my bed, I was into anything and everything. I tried desperately to keep busy. I concentrated on hourly tasks rather than the big picture. Whenever able, I saddled my neighbor into a wheelchair for visits throughout the different wards. I'm not sure which one of us enjoyed it more. The smile on his face did wonders for my own psyche.

I also chipped in at chow time. My arms worked fine, so I set tables and assisted those that couldn't feed themselves. While there, I struck up a friendship with another wounded helper. He was a paratrooper from one of our Airborne Divisions. Like me, he too stayed active and always lent a hand, even with one arm in a sling.

Over time, we grew more familiar with each other and our conversations dug a little deeper. One day, he handed me his X-rays and revealed his story. Before the war, he'd been a small town auto mechanic somewhere in

New York State. Once deposited behind enemy lines, he was to use these skills to coax commandeered enemy equipment into running for our side.

Hours before D-Day, he and his unit fell from their plane into the French countryside. As with most, he landed by himself, well off target. He managed to start an abandoned half-track and soon hooked up with an officer from a different unit. Together, they rolled down a rural road in search of additions to their small party. But instead, a German squad ambushed them along a tree line. The majority of the enemy fire came from the passenger side and killed the American officer instantly. Out of options, the mechanic leaned against his comrade's lifeless body and played dead. Unfortunately, the ruse met only limited success. A single Jerry punched a new clip into his weapon and strode over to the driver's side. Without further warning, he let loose another blast into the pair. The Krauts then moved on, leaving both Americans for dead, but only one was. My friend had survived.

His arm bore the brunt of the enemy burst. Some slugs remained. It was awe inspiring to witness a man once so bullet ridden, laying out silverware.

My Short-lived Drug Addiction

While healing in that hospital, I experienced a bit of another problem. During most days, I hauled my mind far away from what had been. But once alone in my rack, I lay defenseless. I couldn't sleep! The events from my war were all so fresh, really just days old. I came to dread the dark, my dreams and the places that they took me.

My doctor prescribed drugs to get me through the nights. More like knockout pills, they turned me off like a light. In a short time, I became reliant, probably addicted. They were the crutch that I needed and provided me safe passage to dawn. I couldn't imagine life without them.

Yet a week before my scheduled departure, my free ride stopped. All my medications, from painkillers to penicillin were cut off. There was no mollycoddling back in those days. Cold turkey topped the treatment programs and out the door I went. Wrapped in bandages and withdrawal symptoms, I headed to my first replacement depot.

Halfway House

I took up residence at Pheasey Farms Estate. Its sprawling grounds lay north of Birmingham, but south of Walsall. Converted to accommodate GI's on their route back to the front, it served as a halfway house.

I felt considerably better almost immediately, perhaps more mentally than physically. Free from that hospital, my spirit soared. After only a few days, I didn't miss its food, drugs, doctors or anything else about it. I was never so happy to leave a place in all my life.

At Pheasey, the Farm's medical staff continued to care for my wounds. My condition improved daily.

The High Life In Birmingham

Once physically able, I along with several others received a Sunday pass into Birmingham. At 11:00 a.m., two dozen of us gathered at the orderly room for inspection. Staff officers gave us the once-over to make sure we didn't reflect poorly on the U.S. Army. They checked for things like clean-shaven faces, proper uniforms and shined shoes. Our getaway was scheduled from noon to 7:00 p.m. We boarded a 2.5-ton GMC with the canvas top down and barreled for the city.

Downtown Birmingham sat fairly quiet on a Sunday afternoon. We unloaded with strict orders to return by 6:30 p.m., sharp. The group quickly scattered. Each person tended to his own agenda. I hung with a buddy from M Company, another of our walking wounded.

We wandered aimlessly down several streets until we happened on an enormous building, enveloping an entire city block. A sign hanging above the door read "Billiards" with an arrow pointing down the steps. We entered the biggest pool hall I'd ever seen. The basement similarly covered the full block and was filled with nothing but billiard tables.

We played a few games, then went upstairs for some drinks. Bars ran along the outer walls with four beer-pumping stations at each. Still mindful of the thick, dark syrup from Bewdley, I opted for one of the lighter varieties.

My friend wasted little time in vacating his stool to mingle with the local female population. He was a good guy, but invariably, a walking, talking, raging hormone. Most of his thoughts began from below the belt. I stayed on at the bar and struck up a conversation with another wounded acquaintance.

My buddy soon returned with his latest conquest, a fine looking English lass. She invited the three of us to her mother's for a spot of tea. We graciously accepted and walked the six blocks to her family's home. The house was old, but very well-built. They clearly had some bucks.

The young woman excused herself to the kitchen. My friend used the opportunity to draw up his scheme. Unfortunately, I was involved. If things went as planned, he'd be spending the night.

"Wino, you've got to get me through our 6:30 check-in!" he begged.

"How in the hell am I going to do that?" I asked. "I don't know how anything works at the Farm."

"I'm sure you'll figure it out," he reassured me.

Our hostess returned with tea and cakes. After a polite

conversation concerning the war, she excused herself yet again. This time she brought back a large picture of her husband. That's right, her husband! He was a British officer, stationed in Italy.

I almost coughed cake across the room! Where I came from, this sort of exchange was far from typical. I felt uncomfortable just being in the same room, guilty by association. But, my buddy appeared undaunted. Apparently for him, this new revelation wasn't a deal breaker.

He worked the game hard, wiped sweat from his brow continually. You could almost see the smoke wafting from his ears. I suggested that we return to camp because he looked feverish, but he wasn't amused.

The front door opened abruptly and in strolled Grandma, pushing a baby carriage. Our hostess hurried over to lift twins in her arms and introduced us to her babies.

What? If not before, my friend had now seen enough! Her life was far too complicated, even for a player like him. He finally came to his senses and stood to politely lament, "I'm very sorry, but we really must be going."

I almost countered with, "Ah, we got lots of time!" but decided to cut him some slack. We thanked them for their hospitality and hoofed it downtown. We drank another beer and hopped the truck back to the Farm. Within the next few days, my English vacation came to an end. I again moved closer to war.

Chapter 8

Back To The Grind

England to Normandy, France

A Second Landing

We left Pheasey Farm behind and traveled to the coast, where we boarded large transports for our return to France and war. As expected, the second landing varied widely from the first. We descended stairs onto floating causeways that led us right into shore. I didn't even get my feet wet. Yet, the scene proved eerily reminiscent. My boots once again imprinted the hallowed sands. After a several-week respite, I was back.

This time, we poured ashore much nearer to Omaha Beach and immediately climbed single file to the higher ground. We passed by the initial stages of what would become the U. S. Military Cemetery at Normandy. A POW camp on its outskirts provided a ready supply of manual labor. Engineers laid lines and angles, while German prisoners busily dug graves. I left stunned by the enormity of it all. It was difficult to even fathom how many of my comrades were already dead.

Old Versus New

We walked miles to our first replacement depot. It served mess around the clock for hungry soldiers sifting through. After chow, officials pointed us to a nearby field, where we spent the night out under the stars.

Early the next morning, we continued on our way and covered another fifteen to twenty miles. At day's end, we hit a much larger station that serviced, not only the return ing wounded, but also GIs fresh from the States.

U. S. Army Signal Corps Photo, Courtesy National Archives

Amid the hedgerows of Normandy, infantry replacements tear down heavy packs before moving up to the front – July 1944.

In comparison, we believed ourselves better than the new guys or at least deserving of preferential treatment. They hadn't tasted the bitterness of battle, while we were "hardened veterans." Those in charge unfortunately thought otherwise and weren't afraid to tell us as much.

Although not one of the ringleaders, I fell comfortably within the veteran camp. At mess that night, some of our ranks butted their way to the front, thinking it their rightful place in line. In charge, a colonel on horseback quickly responded to remedy the situation.

From his Sam Brown belt to his swagger stick, he was regular army. Familiar with his kind, I kept my mouth shut, but few others followed my lead. Terms like "desk jockey" and "clerk" soon flew randomly from the crowd. That guy got hot immediately! He turned varying shades of red, not from embarrassment, but from anger. Without hesitation, he moved in a company of heavily armed MPs, who quickly forced our herd to one side. This cleared the way for hundreds of replacements to eat ahead of us. We could only watch and wait. By the time we received our food, what little remained was cold, dry and disgusting. That didn't set well with some. What once may have been friction, was now fire.

"Press my demands and I will have no alternative but to order these men to open fire!" the colonel warned.

I'd seen enough to know that I didn't want any part of it. I was there to fight Germans not our own Military Police. Although lower-toned grumbling continued, there was no outright insubordination—at least, at that moment.

Once again, we all bedded down in an open field. Old timers camped on one side of the hedgerow, while the newcomers occupied the other. The remnants of war lay everywhere. Stacks of German equipment, machine guns, rounds of ammunition, silk bags of excess propellant, discarded by artillery units, all littered the scene.

In complete disregard of a blackout order, multiple fires raged on our side of the tree line. Some tempers similarly burned out of control, stoked by a perceived suppertime mistreatment. With darkness settling in, a group of experienced looters helped themselves to the mess stash. They cut holes in the tents and really brought back the booty. The take included gallon cans of everything from hash to pears, not to mention sack after sack of bread.

Yet, that was only the beginning. The picnic soon evolved into a full-blown party, complete with fireworks. Bags of powder first flew into the blazes. Swoosh! The flames leapt toward heaven. Discarded belts of enemy ammo next jumped in. Hot rounds howled in all directions.

In the midst of the revelry, an enemy plane happened high overhead. The pilot noticed the commotion and dropped a 500-pound bomb as a greeting. It landed just on the other side of the hedgerow, but remarkably, did not detonate. It was a dud!

A curious band of us crawled through the brush to check out the bomb. It had dug a significant hole, then buried itself. Tail fins protruded from the mud. Thoughts of what could and should have been made us sick with regret. Humbled by it all, we extinguished the fires. Only the grace of God had spared us from a terrible catastrophe and a lifetime of tortuous guilt.

The next morning, just as the sun peaked over the eastern horizon, a column of trucks pulled into camp. Officers sorted us by unit and ordered all aboard. As we exited, I noticed the colonel sitting on his horse. He seemed to take great pleasure in our departure. No doubt, he ordered the convoy to rid us from his hair. I can't say that I blame him. We granted his wish and rolled on down the line.

Home Again, But The House Was Empty

Trucked southwest, my gang eventually disembarked at a 90th Division depot. After processing, a much smaller group of us took aim at the 358th Command Post.

Additional hours of "hurry up and wait" then saw a few dozen of us onto the 3rd Battalion. I waded through more red tape before finally reporting to M Company. What a bureaucratic nightmare!

I was glad to be back home, but things had changed. When I checked in with the 1st sergeant, it wasn't my old friend, Paul Inman. I learned that he also had been wounded in battle and evacuated from the field. In the next few days, I'd come to know that story all too well.

The new 1st sergeant sent me to company headquarters for reassignment. Now the middle of the night, I stumbled into our makeshift command post, a meager farmhouse. I looked forward to seeing Captain Marsh again. But when the staff woke the officer in charge, I met an unfamiliar face instead.

1st Lieutenant John Mateyko hailed from East Conemaugh, Pennsylvania. He worked the coal mines near Johnstown, prior to war. Drafted in 1941, the high school valedictorian soared through the ranks like a meteor.

1st Lieutenant John Mateyko
M Company, 358th Infantry

As a replacement, he first took over our 3rd Platoon, shortly after my evacuation from Normandy. Thus, I didn't know him at all. At the time of our initial encounter, he was either "M's" executive or commanding officer. He would bounce back and forth between the two positions over the next several months.[1]

Mateyko briefly leaned up from his bed to scan our small crowd and quickly ordered each man back to his former platoon. I fully realized that Captain Marsh's absence most likely meant that he, too, was a casualty of war. In fact, I began to wonder if anyone was left. I was home, but the house was empty. It seemed that everyone I knew was gone. Strangers had taken their places, filled their boots, but it would never be the same again. Yet to find one familiar face, I reported to my new platoon leader and lay down in a ditch until morning.

We rose to find that a thick fog, closely matching my mental state, enveloped the countryside. I even double-checked, just to make sure I was in the right company. Then I caught a glimpse of Sergeant Howard Pemberton. In the last few weeks, he had mended from a bullet wound to the shoulder and returned from England.

Our radio operator, Garold Anderson, was also still with the group. He'd seen it all and fine-tuned the picture for me. Indeed, things were as they appeared. Most all my old friends were gone. Some healed in English hospitals, while others were already back in the States.

Many were in the ground—Eddie Cahill, Rudy Barta, Milford Fagerstrom, Earl Hagerman, Felix Rainosek, Arnold Jackson, Andy Konitzer, Con Kroleski, Freddie Luna, Frank Manning, Frank Music, Walt Sanderson, Frank Turek, Art Gerhardt, Rino Pellegrini, Bob Isenberg, Sam Crisciullo, Henry Jackiewicz, Ev Stallings, Joe Simkewicz.[2] They were all buddies of mine, killed in the weeks I was away.

Czechoslovakian by ancestry, Otto Kutach was the fifth

of ten children, born and raised in Lavaca County, Texas. Before departing to England, he married Miss Helen Cook on May 24, 1943.[3]

In war, he'd been one of the fortunate ones from Amon Hartwick's section. He had survived the 88 shelling in the apple orchard near Picauville with only minor injuries. But on June 16, outside of Gourbesville, enemy snipers pinned down his machine gun squad. When a crewmate was hit and left unprotected, rather than hunker down, Kutach hurried to his aid. In the process, he too was shot. High on the leg, the wound bled badly from the thigh area. He lost a considerable amount of blood before medics could even reach him. Although eventually evacuated to England, he would not recover.[4]

Private First Class Otto Kutach
M Company, 358th Infantry
WIA June 16, 1944 - Died June 22, 1944

Private First Class Otto Kutach died in a British hospital on June 22, 1944. His wife never remarried. Shortly after the war, at the request of the family, Otto's remains were returned to Texas. Today his body rests in Lavaca County's St. Mary's Cemetery.[5]

I'd also heard that my old platoon leader, Lieutenant Rakowski had been wounded, but was thankfully alive. The way he went after war, I can't say that I was surprised.

These men were so brave, so true and maybe most of all, so unselfish. Many were new to our country, yet fought like they owned the place. It was now their country too and they knew it, breathed it, lived it and loved it. Although they weren't names you'd find on the Mayflower's rolls, we won World War II because of men like Ray Krolick, Otto Kutach, and Bruno Rakowski, the sons and grandsons of immigrants. No longer Czechs or Poles, they were Americans and willingly sacrificed all for their newly adopted country. None gave more.

Hill 122 - Hell On Earth

I heard horrific tales of a place called Foret de Mont Castre - Hill 122. Few knew the full story of the battle fought there on July 10-12. Most that had taken part were gone, dead or wounded. The site came to be known by many as "Purple Heart Hill." It all happened while I was away. In my absence, my unit, the 3rd Battalion, 358th Infantry found themselves at the head of it all.

A History of the 90th Division in World War II by 1st Lt. Joe I. Abrams aptly recounted these most difficult of times.

"The dark-shadowed woods of Mont Castre, that day, felt the shock and impact of men who wouldn't be stopped against a line that wouldn't be broken. ...

"...Close range machine-gun fire from carefully concealed positions spread havoc in the 90th's ranks. Grenades came from everywhere, rifle fire spewed from the tangled undergrowth. ...The Americans charged. With hand grenades and bayonets they stormed the line. ...With machine guns blazing from their hips, in spite of wounds and certain death, they charged.

"They dropped and rose and fought again, then dropped again ... and still they fought.

"...Decimated beyond recognition (52% casualties), the Battalion reformed that night as a single group.

"On the following day the Division attacked once more. Weakened as it was, there was no stopping it now. ...The 90th struck and continued to strike until the cream of the enemy's armies, the mighty and invincible parachutists who had scourged the nations of Europe, hesitated, cracked, broke and ran. ..." [6]

U. S. Army Signal Corps Photo, Courtesy National Archives

The 3rd Battalion took up residence in devastated St. Jores, France, prior to its assault on nearby Foret de Mont Castre. Pictured here, the parish priest surveys damage done to the local church and graveyard – July 7, 1944.

The 3rd Battalion

For its courageous efforts, the 3rd Battalion, 358th Infantry earned the rarest of group honors—the Presidential Unit Citation. Our outfit numbered as the first in the entire 90th Division to receive the prestigious award.[7] The citation read in part:

"... The Third Battalion, 358th Infantry, is cited for extraordinary heroism in the face of the enemy in France. During the period 10-12 July 1944, the officers and men of this organization displayed great courage, endurance and dogged determination in the attack through the dense Foret de Mont Castre, France. The position known as the "Mahlman Line" was part of the main enemy defensive line. It consisted of dug-in positions, cunningly camouflaged in the tangled underbrush and other devices which utilized to the fullest the natural defensive qualities of the area. Despite repeated fierce enemy counterattacks the Battalion relentlessly drove forward and eliminated a battalion of parachute infantry and a company of parachute engineers, both of which were part of the elite 5th German Parachute Division. By the end of the first day the Battalion Commander and 11 of the 17 Company officers were casualties but the advance had progressed to within 75 yards of the initial objective. The following day the remnants of the three rifle companies, one of which only had 20 men, were reorganized into one composite company with a strength of 126 men and commanded by a Lieutenant. In a renewed charge the depleted Battalion overran the objective, killed 40 enemy, captured 8 machine guns, bazookas and mortars. On 12 July 1944 as it left the forest the Battalion, retaining its aggressiveness, fought with exceptional daring and great skill and took successive objectives. The Battalion's break through the enemy's main position contributed materially to the Division's advance. The inspiring lead-

ership of its officers and the gallantry displayed by all ranks were in accordance with the highest military traditions. ..." [8]

Colonel Bealke

Battle wise beyond his years or experience, our battalion commander, Lieutenant Colonel J.W. Bealke led the way. For his actions, clearly above and beyond the call to duty, Bill Bealke earned the Distinguished Service Cross.

General George S. Patton, Jr. pinned the Distinguished Service Cross on Colonel J.W. Bealke. Decades later, Bealke still remembered Patton's high-pitched voice, prodding him in jest, "You little bastard! The only reason you're still alive is that you're not big enough for a bullet to hit!" [9] *Bealke only stood 5'6".* [10]

Bealke's DSC citation detailed his heroics:

"... On 10 July 1944, Lieutenant Colonel Bealke, commanding the 3rd Battalion, 358th Infantry 90th Infantry Division, with six men of his battalion headquarters was advancing through the dense undergrowth of the Foret de Mont Castre, France, between his two assault companies. The battalion mission was to clear the forest of the enemy. After advancing some 400 yards into the forest approximately 20 paratroopers from the elite 5th German Parachute Division, attacked fanatically, screaming, throwing hand grenades and firing machine pistols. Colonel Bealke, killed two of the enemy with hand grenades, wounded a third and took two others prisoner. The enemy formation broke. A second German group then attacked from the right flank, but Colonel Bealke killed two with his pistol, one falling at his feet. Twenty additional soldiers arrived as reinforcements just before a third enemy group attacked from the rear of Colonel Bealke's group. Of the 3rd attacking party 3 were killed, 8 taken prisoner and the remainder disappeared. Colonel Bealke then continued advancing through the forest. About 200 yards deeper into the timber, three enemy grenade launcher teams opened fire. Colonel Bealke wounded the German Officer commanding the position, and the rest of his detachment killed, wounded or dispersed the enemy crews. Receiving word by radio that a company of enemy infantry, in column, was proceeding across his front, Colonel Bealke, with an artillery observer and one wireman swung to the left to reach high ground for observation. The observer was wounded and wireman killed. Colonel Bealke laid his own wire line to the observation point and from there directed artillery fire against the enemy column for more than an hour until it was destroyed or dispersed. Throughout this action Colonel Bealke was under heavy mortar and small arms

fire. From the observation post he ordered by radio the reorganization and employment of his Battalion and directed the completion of the mission—occupation of the woods. Through the extraordinary heroism, aggressive leadership and dogged determination, in spite of heavy casualties among his officers and men, Colonel Bealke led his men to a brilliant victory, one of the most outstanding in the operations of his Division in Normandy. ..." [11]

Casualties Everywhere!

Yet, often with extraordinary achievement comes great cost. Such is the case with Foret de Mont Castre, where the price paid in American lives was nothing short of staggering. The vast majority of men in my battalion, some 70%, were battle casualties. The "Daily Battalion Strength Reports," detailing the number of able-bodied soldiers in each company, tell the story. [12]

July 10, 1944		July 13, 1944	
I	114	I	27
K	104	K	13
L	117	L	30
M	129	M	70
	464		140

My old buddy and transportation corporal, Gail Hohman, who had saved the day at Picauville, was severely wounded. An enemy mortar round landed close. The ensuing explosion launched him through the air, while the shrapnel crushed the back of his skull. Remarkably, he survived. Once stabilized, he was evacuated to England, where he spent weeks in bed, blind and paralyzed. He eventually regained his sight and with extensive physical therapy, his movement was restored.

In a matter of months, he was shipped to the States. Doctors at O'Reilly General Hospital in Springfield, Missouri put a plate in the back of his head. After well over a year in and out of different facilities, Gail finally returned home to Kansas, and to his wife, Ruth.[13] His war was over.

I also learned that a man I greatly admired, our company commander, Captain John Marsh was killed in action on Hill 122. I wasn't surprised to hear that he met his end while up front, personally leading his men in battle. He never was one to hide in a basement bunker. Like Colonel Bealke, Captain Marsh earned the Distinguished Service Cross for giving his all at Foret de Mont Castre. The official citation described the action.

"... On 10 July 1944, Captain Marsh was commanding Company "M", 358th Infantry Regiment, advancing against a strong enemy position in the vicinity of the Foret de Mont Castre, France when the rifle companies of the 3rd Battalion became disorganized and separated in the face of intense enemy fire. Captain Marsh, realizing that many of the officers were replacements with little combat experience, left his heavy weapons company in control of the second in command and went forward to assist the battalion commander in organizing a hasty defense. With utter disregard of enemy fire coming from the front and both flanks, he led small groups of riflemen forward to close gaps in the line, boldly directing their fire until the enemy was forced to retire. Before a complete reorganization could be effected, the enemy counter-attacked and again Captain Marsh left his company to proceed to the foremost front line troops to give his assistance. As he directed fire on the enemy he took up arms of the wounded and inspired his men to drive off the enemy. Even after suffering the wounds which resulted in his death he continued to lead his men until he fell, unable to go farther. ..."[14]

Another Story Begins

Captain John Marsh met his wife, Mary "Beth" Edwards in Abilene, Texas, while stationed at Camp Barkeley. In May 1943, they were married in Dallas. When he left for England, Beth, now pregnant with their first child, moved to Billings, Montana to stay with John's dad, Paul.

Captain John Marsh with his wife, Beth and niece Merry, all smiles in Montana, prior to war.

On the morning of his death, Captain Marsh received word, in a letter from his wife, that she'd given birth to a healthy baby boy. Their first and only child, William Joseph Marsh was born on June 24, 1944.[15]

Captain John and Beth Marsh - 1943

On that fateful day in July, at Foret de Mont Castre, 1st Sergeant Paul Inman fought by Marsh's side as a member of his command team. In fact, they were hit with shrapnel from the same enemy mortar round. The blast blew both men to the ground. They lay beside each other, both seriously wounded, when Marsh asked Inman for a drink of water from his canteen. The 1st Sergeant obliged, without hesitation. Far from help, the two aided each other, but Marsh's condition deteriorated rapidly. He was bleeding out and the water had only exacerbated the problem. Although Inman tried desperately, he couldn't save his captain's life. On his deathbed, amid the tangled landscape and sheets of enemy fire, Marsh's thoughts left the battlefield behind to visit a son he'd never see—a son he'd never hold, but a son he surely loved. Accepting his final fate, Captain Marsh turned to his old friend and comrade, 1st Sergeant Paul Inman and whispered in defiant glory, "They may get me, but they won't get my boy!" And then, he died.[16]

When Beth received word of her husband's death, she was understandably devastated. In his honor, she changed their infant son's name to John Weldin Marsh, Jr.[17]

One Man's Mission

Born and raised poor in Canyon, Texas, Paul Inman was one of seven children. When his father died young, his mother married a man with ten kids of his own. Now one of seventeen, he realized early on that there wasn't room for him. At age fourteen, he moved to a nearby dairy farm, where he lived and labored seven days a week to send money home to his family.

He enlisted in the service in 1936, at a time when the Army was less respected, far from revered. With tough-minded tenacity and a tireless work ethic, he rapidly ascended through the ranks. By the time war called, he was a well-groomed leader of men.

Yet, perhaps even more than his metal, Inman possessed a softer side. He was compassionate, and truly cared for those with which he served, especially his captain.

After a lengthy stay in an English hospital, Inman recovered from his wounds and returned to the front. But, he was forever changed. He would not forgot Captain Marsh, what he had said, nor the wife and son he left behind. It became Inman's lifelong mission to locate them—to tell a boy of the father he never knew.

1st Sergeant Paul Inman
M Company, 358th Infantry

Following war, he searched Billings, but with no luck. By then, Beth and John, Jr. had already moved back to Texas. Discouraged, yet steadfast in his resolve, Inman refused to give up. As he grew old and his own sons matured, he shared the stories with them. His commitment became theirs.

Beth Marsh died in 1990, from cancer. Sadly, Paul Inman passed away in 2000, never having fulfilled the goal of finding his captain's son. Yet, his boys knew how much it all meant to him. As a right of passage, in honor of their father, they collectively continued the search.[18]

In 2004, 1st Sergeant Paul Inman's son, Wade contacted Captain John Marsh's son, John Jr. Amazingly, they only lived a few hours apart. Through the words of his father, Wade Inman poured out all he knew of Captain John Marsh. Emotions ran high. Although he'd never met his dad, John Jr. came to know him. A gentleman, an officer, a husband and maybe most of all, a father— Captain John Marsh meant much to many. In his dad's dying words, a son heard his father speak for the first and last time. After sixty years, John Marsh, Jr. learned that as a baby boy, he was not only loved by the father that war took away, but also consumed his final thoughts on earth. The news was well worth the wait.[19]

May We Never Forget

Although now just names on stones or pages in a book, fallen friends live on in my memory. I see them today as I last saw them in early June 1944—mugs alive with ornery grins and bright eyes wide-open. Some might call it strange, but I hope their smiling faces never leave me. I prefer to remember them that way.

And these were but a few. The hedgerows of Normandy dealt a savage blow to American families. Parents lost sons, wives lost husbands, children lost fathers. Max Hastings in his book, *Overlord, D-Day and The Battle For Normandy* paid particular attention to the utter devastation within my group. He wrote, *"... It had become brutally apparent to every man in First Army that service in an infantry unit was an almost certain sentence to death or wounds. ... The unfortunate 90th Division suffered replacement of 150 percent of its officers and over 100 percent of enlisted men in its first six weeks in action. ..."*[20]

For the most part, we were now a new outfit. The old had done what was asked of it and sacrificed much in passing the baton to the next in line. It was time to pick up the pieces and move on, back to the grind.

Chapter 9

Our Breakout and Beyond

Cathelmais to Le Mans, France

Off We Go

Part of operation COBRA, extensive carpet-bombing runs softened German positions. With the field prepped, American forces broke from the Cotentin Peninsula. Under such pressure, many enemy outfits fled the scene in a hasty retreat.

For speed's sake, we loaded onto trucks and became motorized. With Jerry momentarily missing in action, we wheeled through one French city after another, almost entirely unencumbered. Periers, Cathelmais, Coutances, Gavray, la Haye Pesnel and Avranches all passed in our wake.[1] In one brief ride through the countryside, we covered more ground than we had gained in the previous two months of fighting. I liked this new look of war. But, would it remain?

Ready For The Worst

We met some pockets of resistance, but nothing significant. Unsure of the enemy's location, our higher-ups grew anxious. They always liked to see a village or two ahead, just to be safe.

With so many recent replacements, I numbered among the few with actual recon experience. Fresh in from my English vacation, I accepted the challenge. It was time to punch the clock and get back to work.

This particular project was far from typical. Potentially, we had many miles to cover and chose to ride, rather than walk. I received orders to take three heavily armed jeeps into enemy territory—the deeper, the better. Top brass wanted a feel for what was out there. For my sake, I sincerely hoped nothing.

Daylight reconnaissance work often proved little more than a dressed-up suicide run. You basically traveled through no-man's land until you made enemy contact. "Contact" could run the gamut from an undetected glance to a full-blown shootout. As for this mission, with jeeps loaded for bear, the latter seemed more likely.

Besides myself, I selected eleven men, four per jeep. We hastily mounted .50-caliber machine guns in each and scattered boxes and belts of ammo about the floors. We laid the windshields down to crisscross bazookas over the hoods, with one weapon aimed at each roadside. Drivers rested Thompson submachine guns on their laps.

At that point, we held a surplus of BARs. Lots of them! I dearly loved that weapon. It had so much more ass than a carbine or even an M1. Its biggest drawbacks were weight and mobility. Not only was the gun heavy, but carrying the ammo could turn the most virile young trooper into a bent-back old man in no time.

Just to try something, we sawed off a few of the barrels. They wouldn't be as accurate, but shooting from a speeding jeep wasn't exactly target practice anyway. In fact, we longed to splatter shells in large swathes and could use a little more spray to our fire. The war was about making do with what you had—improvisations for survival.

Packed to the brim, we must have resembled a well-stocked weapons dealer. The jeep floors were so awash in ammo that we barely found room for our feet. We angled southeast from Avranches, ready for the worst.

Show Time!

Our destinations were small in size, no more than villages. I don't believe I ever knew their names. If I did, they left me long ago.

Much like decoys, we made no attempt to sneak or hide. With the Germans on the run, we aimed to lure them out into the open, where our greater unit could get a better whack at them. We would be the aggressors—strike before struck upon. Getting away clean would be the catch. We approached the first burg and I huddled my men for the game plan.

"We're flying through these towns!" I shouted. "Give them everything we've got! BARs on the second stories, 50s on the firsts! Drivers, do not stop or slow down until we're out! Heads up for Frenchies! Now, let's go!"

At top speed, we painted the buildings with bullets. You just can't imagine the firepower we possessed in those three jeeps. After exiting out the other side, we took a look back. Clouds of brick dust wafted into the sky. The main drag had appeared completely vacant. We scratched "town one" from our list—so far, so good.

A safe distance away, we stopped for gun maintenance. To keep our weapons singing a smooth song, each vehicle carried gun oil. Many of us were farm boys and knew well the importance of proper lubrication. Some of those cowboys from places like Wyoming, Texas and Oklahoma worked magic with a little bailing wire and a bit of the black stuff. We really juiced those receivers.

Dry guns meant dead soldiers.

The next village grew in size, but we stuck with the same strategy. I immediately noticed German jeeps, trucks and then men. We caught them napping, completely unawares. Clearly, they weren't expecting well-armed visitors.

We hammered away, but I was startled to see multiple aircraft engines chained up from hoists. These guys were Luftwaffe Maintenance! No wonder they weren't prepared to fight! Why they were that close to the front, I'll never know. Apparently, no one told them about the race to the motherland.

They paid dearly for their lack of readiness. We inflicted heavy damage on that small enemy force. Although some returned fire, it was token at best. We neither slowed down nor suffered any casualties.

Maybe a mile out of town, we turned right at the first crossroads. We needed a little time to let the air settle, to reload and re-lube. Still within view of the main road, we pulled our jeeps into a field under a nice big tree. In tidying up, we swept out onto the ground all the spent shell casings and empty ammo cans. We again readied our weapons for action, but the grassy shade below that beautiful tree kept calling our names. Ah, why not? We all sprawled out onto the lush natural carpeting to forget about the war for a few minutes. There was nothing quite like lying in the grass, daydreaming of home, miles behind enemy lines.

Unexpected Brush With Royalty

The 90th Division was switched from First to Third Army. On August 1, 1944, General George S. Patton, Jr. took command.[2] In all honesty, it didn't mean that much to me. I had heard a couple of Patton's speeches in England, knew of his reputation, but figured I'd never actually see him while in war. After all, generals typically worked far from the battlefield. I'd soon find out that Patton was anything but typical.

General George S. Patton, Jr.

Oddly enough, the blasts from an air horn, not machine guns, broke the tranquil silence and so rudely interrupted our siesta. At first, we regarded the cries with amusement. But as they increased in volume, we became a little more than curious. The sounds of vehicles bumping down the main road soon accompanied the trumpet calls.

"Who in the hell has an air horn on their jeep?" I joked with a buddy.

We stepped out from under the tree just in time to witness the caravan pass through the intersection. Two American jeeps led the way, followed by an armored car. A ton of antennas with attached streamers poked from its top.

We all stood, stared and chuckled nervously as they blew by our locale. When the three screeched to a halt, so did the laughter. My stomach turned somersaults as I watched them back into the crossroads and speed toward us.

One of the jeeps stopped right in front of me, not more than a few feet from my boots. I now clearly noticed two large silver air horns on the hood and a red license plate with three gold stars attached to the front bumper. Concern pitched to panic when I recognized King George himself, General Patton, step from the vehicle. Uh, oh!

If only by a few days, we were now his men. I assumed that he was a little lost, being that far forward. But over the next several months, I'd learn that he often graced the front lines with his presence. He was probably there checking up on his new rank and file. Judging by our predicament, it promised to be a poor showing.

He paced to my position and barked, "Who's in charge of this recon?"

Visibly shaken, I replied, "I am Sir."

"Can you tell me, Sergeant, why you're stopped here, sunning yourselves in this ditch?" he questioned.

"To regroup and reload, Sir," I fumbled.

"Bullshit!" he spat, only inches away from my face.

In a profanity-laced tirade, he lit me up! Expletives flew like confetti at a tickertape parade! Yeah, I was embarrassed, but the berating sparked a defiant nerve. Yeah, I had plenty of room for improvement. But then, frontline kids needed to lie in the grass and dream of home every once in awhile.

After handing my ass back to me, he and his entourage reversed to the intersection, then motored toward

Avranches. We initially set a course for the next village, but after several miles, just called it off. Now hours into enemy territory, there just wasn't anything there. The German left flank was nowhere to be found. With American men and equipment already in motion, our little recon didn't much matter anymore. As the 90th Division rolled our way, around the enemy's unprotected west, we backtracked to meet them, hoping to avoid another run-in with you know who.

Meeting With McHolland

We rejoined our unit without fanfare. Patton hadn't reported the encounter, so we didn't either. Although now once again on foot, we continued an accelerated pace to the southeast. At times, we covered twenty-five miles in a day—no easy task in the blistering summer heat. St. Hilaire du Harcouet, Landivy and St. Suzanne all quickly fell by the wayside with little resistance.[3]

U. S. Army Signal Corps Photo, Courtesy National Archives

The 90th Infantry Division passes through the ruins of Mayenne, France, en route to St. Suzanne - August 1944.

U. S. Army Signal Corps Photo, Courtesy National Archives

The 90th Infantry Division passes through the ruins of Mayenne, France, en route to St. Suzanne - August 1944.

I took charge of a machine-gun section on our battalion's right flank. On one memorable occasion, we stopped at a T-road intersection. Per orders, I fanned out my crews and positioned their guns with excellent fields of fire. But due to our ceaseless movement, I chose not to dig them in. It was a decision I'd shortly come to regret.

1st Lieutenant Robert McHolland pulled up in a jeep. I'd known him a long time and liked him much. Everyone did. His personality meshed well with the average Joe or GI. Respected and well-loved by the troops, he was a man's man, who didn't play games or put on airs—just took care of business.

Raised country, he hailed from rural Hurley, Missouri. His father died when he was just fourteen and his mother followed seven years later. As the second youngest of six children, he and his siblings learned to make do with less. From these humble roots, he gained the perspective and common sense that would lead him so capably into battle.

1st Lieutenant Robert McHolland
M Company, 358th Infantry

Robert graduated from Hurley High School in 1938 to attend State Teachers College, now Southwest Missouri State University. After two years of training, he taught in the region's one-room schoolhouses.

He also became involved in the Citizen's Military Training Corps (CMTC). When war broke out, he was commissioned a second lieutenant. After stints at Camp Wolters, Texas and Fort Benning, Georgia, he was assigned to the 90th Division at Camp Barkeley.[4]

Maybe more than anything else, McHolland had a quiet charisma about him. While many officers clamored just to hear the sound of their own voices, he chose his words sparingly. Consequently, when he spoke, everyone listened.

I assumed that he wanted to talk of our next objective. To orchestrate movements between heavy weapons sections and rifle units, the officers in our battalion often straddled platoon and company lines.

Yet on that occasion, I was wrong. For not digging in my guns, McHolland read me the riot act. I privately wondered if I had a sign attached to my ass reading, "Chew here!" Between him and Patton, they left little for anyone else.

"Sir, as fast as we're moving, we don't have time to dig in!" I respectfully argued. "We'll be out of here in an hour!"

"Don't give me that, Sergeant!" he shouted. "Anytime we stop, I want your men digging in! This is a standing order that I expect to be followed! It's for your own good! Got it?"

I got it, and shut my trap. Just then, an explosion near an old farmhouse down the lane changed the subject.

"Let's you and I go check that out," McHolland ordered, nodding at me.

We grabbed a handful of men from my squad and ran to the scene. We immediately noticed an American jeep parked by the back door. Still smoldering, it had taken a direct hit. While we scanned the surroundings, a group of Germans popped from the house and scurried toward the woods. They had greater numbers, but thankfully didn't stick around to find out. We willingly sprayed fire into their backsides and even downed a couple. I wasn't sorry to see them go as they disappeared into the forest, and we didn't pursue.

We approached the jeep to find its two occupants mangled beyond all recognition. Thrown by the blast, the driver's lifeless frame draped the vehicle's hood. The bottom half of a soldier sat in the passenger seat, his upper torso gone. After a quick search, I turned up an empty helmet adorned with captain's bars. Most likely, a panzerfaust dealt the damage. It was the German equivalent to our bazooka, but twice as effective.

These two weren't from our unit. I'm sure they'd taken a wrong turn somewhere—maybe back around Omaha Beach. The mistake cost them their lives. The best we could do for them was to notify the grave registration people.

Mac and I returned to the intersection and bid each other farewell. There were no hard feelings. That wasn't the first time, nor would it be the last that he straightened me out. I probably needed it. And in some ways, I'm sure his advice helped me survive.

Weapon Gone Awry

We moved out of this area within the hour and headed south. Dusk neared, so we halted for the night. Time passed quietly until about 1:00 a.m., when a runner summoned me from my foxhole.

Clearly troubled, he panted, "Sergeant Winebrenner, please report to our command post immediately! Please hurry!"

I grabbed my gear and trailed him down the path. With no moonlight, deep darkness shrouded our way. We soon arrived at our CP, nothing more than a small shack. Per usual, blankets blacked out all light attempting to escape from windows and doors. I entered on a scene I'll never forget. I initially couldn't believe my eyes. Bloodied Americans, "M's" leadership covered the floor as screams for "Medic!" flew in all directions.

I learned that it was this same runner who had inadvertently caused the damage. He'd been carrying an anti-tank grenade on the end of his rifle. Worse yet, without the safety engaged! When he set his weapon down in the corner, the blank cartridge fired to propel the grenade into the ceiling where it exploded upon impact. Confined to such a small area, the ensuing shrapnel storm proved exceedingly violent, not to mention the concussion. Many lay wounded, some already dead.

A runner had no business with an anti-tank grenade. It was mindless overkill, a surefire recipe for disaster! This tragedy should have never been, but you couldn't babysit everybody.

Those grenades never lived up to their billing anyway, caused more harm than good. We most often used them for fishing. One dropped into a stream really brought up dinner. Not worth a damn against enemy tanks, they were hell on trout.

For a breath of fresh air, 1st Lieutenant Mateyko had exited the structure only minutes before the catastrophe. The well-timed act not only spared him from certain injury, but also likely saved his life. Divine intervention? Most definitely, if you ask him.[5]

We all felt fortunate that he was unharmed. I hadn't known him long, but could already tell that he was a keeper. Brave, savvy, intelligent, personable and morally sound, Mateyko was someone that we could follow. Whether officially in charge or not, from that moment on, he was our leader and "M" was his company.

The next morning, we moved out as if nothing had happened. Guys asked questions, but didn't get answers. Believe me, they were better off not knowing. In a few days, we received much needed replacements—several officers, a few non-coms and twenty some privates. I'd been operating as 1st sergeant since the accident, but relinquished that role for the permanent reconnaissance position.

Chapter 10

Closing The Gap

Alencon to Chambois, France

Setting The Stage

We forged ahead at such a brisk pace that we knowingly left entire enemy units behind. The German 7th Army soon surfaced well in our wake and attempted to retake the town of Mortain. In an effort to cut us off, they wreaked havoc thoughout regions to our rear. [1]

Near Le Mans, we stopped our push to Paris and instead, angled north through Alencon. With this abrupt change in direction, we sensed that something was up—something big. Combined Allied forces simultaneously drove the enemy south from Caen and east from Mortain. Retreating German outfits all funneled toward Falaise, France.[2] Strategists estimated their size at hundreds of thousands of men, not to mention all of their equipment. The enormity of the potential encounter raised the stakes to new heights.

In fact, the situation was so noteworthy that it warranted a rare message from the Supreme Allied Commander.[3] On August 14, 1944, he penned,

"… To all soldiers, sailors, and airmen – through your combined skill, valor and fortitude, you have created in France a fleeting but definite opportunity for a major Allied victory. One whose realization will mean notable progress toward the final downfall of our enemy. … Because the victory we can now achieve is infinitely greater than any it has been so far possible to accomplish in the West and because this opportunity may be grasp only through the utmost zeal, determination, and speedy action, I make my present appeal to you more urgent than ever before. I request every airman to make it his direct responsibility that the enemy is blasted unceasingly by day and by night and is denied safety either in flight or in plight. I request every sailor that no part of the hostile forces can either escape or be reinforced by sea and that our comrades on the land want nothing that guns and ships and ship's companies can bring them. I request every soldier to go forward to his assigned objective with a determination that the enemy can survive only through surrender. Let no foot of ground once gained be relinquished nor a single German escape through a line once established.

"With all of us resolutely performing our special tasks, we can make this week a momentous one in the history of this War; a brilliant and fruitful week for us, a fateful one for the ambitions of the Nazi tyrants."

Signed;
Dwight D. Eisenhower

Targets To Spare

American and British planes strafed and bombed our fleeing enemy, while artillery hammered them from the high ground. The Germans clawed desperately at escape. Nearly surrounded, they charged hard for the one way out, the last hole in the snare. The 90th Division raced to fill the gap. We lunged north at top speed as our Polish and Canadian counterparts surged south. Yet, could our forces connect in time?

We in 3rd Battalion hurried northeast from Argentan. We started catching fire near le Bourg St. Leonard, but continued on to positions north of Chambois. Although we knew the Poles and Canadians were close, we failed to completely bridge the gap. A small leak remained open between our forces. But out of time, it would have to suffice.

After expelling the enemy from the high ground, we set up shop. Colonel Bealke scattered a mix of machine gunners and riflemen throughout the immediate area. We blocked all roads exiting that patch of the Falaise pocket, north by northeast of Chambois.

Per orders, I dug in with two heavy machine guns. A 57mm anti-tank gun and crew soon joined us. Others gathered nearby. The elevated vantage point offered a truly textbook field of fire.

We didn't wait long. In less than an hour, the enemy arrived. A group of ordnance trucks led the way. We held our greeting until they closed; then we tore into the first few. With drivers dead or wounded, vehicles barreled along aimlessly. Many crashed into each other. The pile-up forced the rear trucks to the outside, yet there wasn't anywhere for them to go. We laid waste to the entire lot, but it was only the beginning.

Jeeps, half-tracks, tanks and lines upon lines of enemy infantry continued to wind through the wreckage and test our metal. We answered every challenge with sheets of bullets and bazooka rounds. Anyone and everyone not hauling ammo or feeding a machine gun, fired something. Our weapons rattled on by the hour, without remission. My hands and fingers were so twisted and cramped. My arms ached. Yet, we dared not rest. There were targets to spare, more by the minute.

U. S. Army Signal Corps Photo, Courtesy National Archives

Burned-out enemy armor flank the streets of a battle-weary Chambois, France - August 1944.

It Went Both Ways

Although the encounters were largely one-sided, we suffered casualties as well. Saco, Maine's Allan McInnis had recently returned from an English hospital. We'd been hit on the same day, back in Normandy. North of Chambois, shrapnel from an exploding enemy round wounded him once more. Again Britain bound, McInnis already had two Purple Hearts to show for his short stay in World War II.[4]

At times, we teetered on the verge of being overrun. Like high tide, a sea of Krauts flooded our emplacements. Savage, close-in fighting ensued. Enemy armor especially proved troublesome.

Multiple German tanks stormed Lieutenant Mateyko's section of the line. At such close range, the enemy machine guns shredded his ranks, while their 88 cannon shells simply cut soldiers in two. In the face of the onslaught, Mateyko attempted to steady his group, but they soon faltered. As GIs raced for the rear, he bravely held his ground. He grabbed a discarded bazooka and dropped to a prone position. While under extremely heavy fire, he disabled three opposing tanks, one right after the other. Inspired by their leader's courage, his men rallied. Together they squelched what remained of the enemy surge.[5]

Mateyko was a modest sort. He would shoulder the responsibility for his unit's shortcomings, rather than blame them. Similarly, when good things happened, he always credited his men, not himself. But at Chambois, try as he might, he couldn't escape the personal accolades. Too many Americans, including our battalion commander, Colonel Bealke, had witnessed his heroic actions. Like it or not, Mateyko rightfully received a Silver Star for courageously holding the line against enemy armor at Falaise.

A Matter Of Faith

More than ever, I began to realize that there was something very special about John Mateyko. He possessed the uncanny ability to pull through the worst imaginable, and not only alive, but also, unscathed. He had side-stepped the disaster at our CP by seconds, just a few short weeks ago, only to come here and go toe to toe with three Kraut tanks. And win! Unbelievable!

Mateyko will be the first to admit that he wasn't lucky—

he was blessed. Luck had a randomness about it, whereas his faith did not. "The good Lord took care of me from beginning to end," he humbly confessed. "Some of those situations that I lived through—I knew He was with me, so I just didn't worry about it. I put my life in His hands." [6]

General James Van Fleet presents
1st Lieutenant John Mateyko with the Silver Star.

Two's A Crowd

During a brief lull in the action, our always-inquisitive 3rd Battalion Surgeon, Doc Bulger nosed through some of the German wreckage. A dead Kraut driver sat in the front seat of a disabled, nondescript two-door sedan. But in the backseat, our good doctor discovered several briefcases. Curious, he opened one to find it packed full of baby-blue bills—1,000 Franc, French notes. Perhaps he'd stumbled onto a German Division's payroll.

A life of luxury, early retirement, a debt-free, Stateside

medical practice—the possibilities seemed endless. But just then, an uninvited visitor peered over his shoulder. Our man of the cloth, Chaplain Joseph Esser abruptly interrupted Bulger's wistful glimpse into a privileged future. "You have to turn that in to Regiment!" Esser counseled.[7] So much for Doc's big dreams! He'd have to work for a living after all.

While at Chambois, Doc also made a house call. Summoned from his aid station, he grabbed his bag on the fly. A villager was in labor and Doc delivered the baby. He tied the cord with a bandage roll, wrapped the baby in a blanket and then returned to war.[8] All in a day's work for a country doctor or battalion surgeon!

3rd Battalion Surgeon,
Captain Richard "Doc" Bulger

Our First German General

Throughout the hours and days, the stacks of smoldering Kraut equipment steadily increased in volume. It became difficult for the newcomers to even find a way through. Faced with this tangled jungle and their own destruction, less hardy enemy soldiers often greeted us with white flags and raised hands. So began our stockpile of prisoners. We'd take an obscene number of POWs before it was all over.

U. S. Army Signal Corps Photo, Courtesy National Archives

Lines of German POWs, captured at the Falaise Gap, wait to be processed in the nearby town of Sees, France - August 1944.

Our heap continued to gain mass. The flow of likely suitors waned to a trickle. Yet early one morning, an enemy command car attempted to plow through. Leave it to a general to believe himself above the fray. Instead of escaping, he drove right into our crosshairs.

At this late stage in the game, to conserve ammunition and keep our guns cool, we switched targets back and forth with the anti-tank crew. Although it was our turn, these guys got so excited at seeing the touring car that they put a shell into its hood before we could even lick our lips. The burst separated the entire front end from the rest of the vehicle. The driver and front-seat passenger were killed instantly.

We held our fire long enough to witness the rear-side door open. Out popped a German general. From his brown knee-length boots to the cap with the small visor, he looked to be regular army. And man, was he mad! He must have been expecting special VIP treatment, but the red carpet had been rolled up long ago. Much to his dismay, we just parked his ass in line with the rest of the prisoners.

Four of us charged the car to scavenge for goodies. Equipped with three rows of seats, tandem wheels in the back and a trunk the size of Texas, she was a sweet ride. Who knew what a general might carry? He was the first we'd experienced.

The treasure hunt failed to live up to expectations. For a man of importance, he didn't have squat. I remember a case in the trunk full of nice silverware, but what would a bunch of grubby old GIs do with that? I did manage to liberate a nice leather map case bearing his initials. After turning over its contents, I wrapped it up and mailed it home to Mom. It's still with me today. Sometimes I pull it out, think back to this guy and laugh. I guess he was just so full of himself that there wasn't room for anything else.

Battalion CP caught wind of our esteemed guest and dispatched a jeep and driver to pick him up. The general pitched such a fit that we placed him atop the hood, much like an ornament. His feet rested on the front bumper.

With things winding down, I accompanied the vehicle back to Battalion and guarded the prisoner from the passenger seat. Much like the rest of us, the jeep driver soon tired of this guy's mouth and purposely hit every pothole on our path. Bumped to and fro, Jerry worried more about his hat than anything else. We couldn't help but laugh.

I spotted something in a nearby hedgerow. While the driver watched the general, I flushed out another German. He was a master sergeant from a Luftwaffe unit who surrendered without incident. Again, it seemed strange to find these oddball outfits at the front, but they were probably more shocked than we were.

I gave him the once-over. He didn't even have a weapon. However, his front shirt pocket held a pay book, filled with a few French francs. I sent them home to Mom, along with the map satchel. I guess you could call them the spoils of war. On the hood he went, as we resumed our bounce toward headquarters.

Meet Our Colonel

Our Battalion CP worked from a two-story structure. Except for a missing portion of its roof, the building was in fairly good condition. As we pulled in, I noticed rows of stretcher-bound wounded, no doubt a mix of GIs and German prisoners.

Colonel Bealke marched our way as we rolled to a stop. "What have you got, Sergeant?" he asked.

"I think he's a Kraut general, Sir, and an angry one at that," I answered.

On cue, this guy starts berating Colonel Bealke up one side and down the other. Bad move! Although short in stature, Bealke was absolutely no one to mess with. I cringed, fully aware that whatever the German gave our colonel, he'd get back tenfold.

Colonel J.W. Bealke
3rd Battalion, 358th Infantry

When Bealke pulled out his sidearm, I sincerely believed that the loud-mouthed Jerry's seconds were numbered. But instead, our colonel used the pistol's butt to emphasize his point. He heatedly explained to the enemy officer matters of proper POW etiquette. At long last, the man got the message and finally accepted that he was no longer in charge. Now quiet as a church mouse, the Kraut commander was transported to Division Headquarters, without a peep in protest.

To The Foot Of Our Door

I lingered on for some food and fresh water. I wandered to the rear of the building and sat in the shade. While enjoying a cool drink, I passed the time with some of the wounded. Then, wham! A huge chunk of the wall blew out the back!

Several enemy tanks and half-tracks, accompanied by infantry had somehow sidled their way along the road in front of our Battalion CP, completely unnoticed. Their cannon shells pierced the building, from front to back. They tore massive holes all the way through. The structure exploded in all directions, materials flew everywhere. Some wounded lay helpless, partially buried by debris.

To our left, the lane became decidedly more sunken. In fact, it dropped deep enough to pause the enemy tank fire. Colonel Bealke stood out front and directed traffic. I remember hearing him scream, "The first man that gets me a tank, I'm making a sergeant! Go! Go! Go!"

Frenzied GIs charged to the top of these roadside ridges. They relentlessly poured in round after round. The large caliber MG and bazooka teams really hit them hard. Well-placed fire blew the tracks on the first few vehicles to trap the rest behind.

Enemy infantry spilled from their trucks to return fire. They tried to take cover on and around their rolling tanks and half-tracks. For many, it became their death trap. Understandably distracted, several didn't notice the logjam in front and were crushed between or pancaked beneath their own vehicles.

The melee only intensified as opposing sides frantically traded fire at close range. We must have had a dozen bazookas in there. They threw shells from all angles. In such chaos, you weren't safe from your own men, let alone the enemy. I recall one GI who caught the tail fin of a friendly round across the side of his face. Although his cheek was sliced wide-open, he clearly could have had it a lot worse.

Now carrying a M1, I battled as best I could, but my total output paled in comparison with that of our machine gun crews. They dealt untold damage. I saw multiple sections, like scythes on wheat, mow down line after line of Kraut soldiers. With all of their tanks and most of their half-tracks now destroyed, the surviving enemy infantry-men surrendered. We ceased fire in time to capture what seemed like hundreds of prisoners.

While clearing the junked German vehicles, I wit-nessed unimaginable carnage. Dozens of bodies, flat-tened by tank treads, carpeted the lane. They literally popped under such immense pressure. Just when you thought you'd seen the worst, something new and even more unsettling always appeared.

Looking Back

A History of the 90th Division in World War II makes note of our Division's numbers at Falaise. *"In a period of four days it had taken more than 13,000 prisoners, killed or wounded an estimated 8,000 of the enemy, but itself suffered less than 600 casualties. More than 300 enemy tanks, 250 self-propelled guns, 164 artillery pieces, 3,270 vehicles, and a variety of other types of equipment and weapons were destroyed. ..."* [9]

U. S. Army Signal Corps Photo, Courtesy National Archives

Interested onlooker and Supreme Allied Commander, Dwight D. Eisenhower examines the carnage near Chambois - August 1944.

Although it was a monumental Allied victory, I hold few fond memories of the fighting at Falaise. It reminded me of a slaughter pen. The scene was not for the faint of heart. We ended so many lives and there they lay, piled up for days before our very eyes. Dead bodies and horse cadavers covered the wreckage, road and nearby fields. The air reeked of death, polluted by thousands of burned and bloated corpses. The stench was nauseating, almost unbearable, surely unforgettable. Time hasn't taken it away. Sure, it was war and there wasn't any way around it, but human beings weren't wired to kill that way—on that grand a scale. In the end, I guess better them than us.

U. S. Army Signal Corps Photo, Courtesy National Archives

Typical Chambois vista, where mangled trucks and rotting corpses blanketed the roads and fields - August 1944.

In Hot Pursuit

Because we failed to interlock lines with our Polish and Canadian counterparts, enemy remnants escaped. Some blamed Bradley, while others faulted Montgomery. Whichever the case, Patton was furious! He eyed checkmate, only to watch it slip through his fingers, across the Seine River.[10] Those Germans fortunate enough to escape, hurried for home, able to fight another day. Unfortunately, we'd meet them again, at places like Metz, France and the Battle of the Bulge. After a brief respite, we pressed east in hot pursuit.

U. S. Army Signal Corps Photo, Courtesy National Archives

In search of more game, an American tank destroyer winds through the Falaise Gap wreckage - August 1944.

Chapter 11

A New Man!

Nemours to Gravelotte, France

Fighting Back

Whether by truck or on foot, we hustled through France. Enemy fighter planes occasionally showered us with attention. But few and far between, they never amounted to much. By early September 1944, the Luftwaffe had fallen from a feared adversary to a general nuisance. Hundreds of thousands of American infantrymen humped along the open roads, fully exposed to aerial assaults that largely never came.

When they did, only one or two enemy aircraft typically braved the skies at a time. With experience, we developed ways to fight back. They brought their planes in low and strafed down our lines. We scattered for cover. But after these initial runs, the pilots banked their fighters and returned for a gander at damage done—always a mistake. We took to the offensive on these secondary flybys. While on a route march, several of us maintained a clip of tracers in our weapons and set our gun sights at five hundred yards. When the time arrived, the others knew to follow our fire.

To grab a better look, the German airmen invariably tipped one wing up and the other down. This made for a real nice target. I aimed at least five lengths ahead, then let loose my clip of tracers. The others fired at the illuminated rounds. Before long, the entire 3rd Battalion spat small arms flak at Jerry's plane. We even smoked a few, which boosted morale immeasurably.

No Gas?

We bypassed Paris to the south through Nemours, then stopped in the vicinity of Reims. Quite literally, the Third Army ran out of gas. With no fuel, we sat for a week, but no one seemed to mind. I know that I didn't.

How could we run out of gas? I've often wondered what really happened and over the years have heard many ideas. Some believe Montgomery to our north got all the juice. The squeakiest wheel gets the grease and Montgomery sure made a lot of noise. Others contend that at such an accelerated pace, we simply outdistanced our supply lines. Or perhaps politics played a part. It was almost election time back in the States. Relative inaction rated far better than a bitter, bloody defeat as we jumped into Germany, and America headed to the polls. Whatever the case, near Reims, we slowed to a crawl. Empty fuel tanks ended Patton's dream of Berlin by Christmas.

The Ammo Heist

In Army Infantry, the poor quality of the ammunition really chapped our ass! At the bottom of the scale, the ball variety jammed and misfired regularly. Yet, that's exactly what they issued to the men who counted on it most.

The armor-piercing rounds topped the heap, by far the finest. However, we rarely saw them. Sure, it made sense that armored units would get armor-piercing shells, but why not make enough for all of us? It caused some hard feelings and even a little jealousy on our part, toward our tanker brethren.

Whether true or not, we believed ourselves short-changed when compared to the armored outfits. Not only did their food look tastier, but also, their clothes were better. They all had these really cool jackets! Plus, the best ammo? Come on! Where's the justice? In our minds, within Patton's Third Army, armor was the favorite son, while infantry was the ugly stepchild.

Or perhaps, we just wanted the best of both worlds. We loved the tankers during the day—the more, the merrier. They did damage that we could only dream of. They were always welcome, wherever we went, whatever we were doing.

But at night, we'd rather they stayed elsewhere. They attracted enemy artillery like a magnet. Do the math. What's the more valuable target—ten grunts or ten tanks? No matter how many times we tried to ditch them, they always seemed to follow. They appreciated our perimeter protection. Blanketed by infantry, they worried less about a satchel charge down the hatch. It was certainly a give-and-take relationship; neither could have won the war without the other.

As for the armor-piercing ammunition, our small group arrived at a general consensus—unspoken, but understood. Whenever the opportunity presented itself, we would do whatever it took to get our hands on that stuff. If that at times meant liberating cases from other friendly units, so be it. Daily, our lives were on the line and we needed a good round too. We reasoned that they could always get more from Ordnance, but we couldn't.

One day, while on flanking patrol near Verdun, we happened on an armored supply train. Unmanned and parked along the roadside, the trucks sat ripe for the picking. A field away, the drivers worked through a chow line. We quietly approached the vehicles and peered into their beds—poor kids with noses pressed to the rich man's window.

After several disappointments, we found an entire 2.5-ton truck packed full of armor-piercing ammo. It was meant to be! We had to have it! With no one around, we hopped in, started her up and drove away nice and easy. Once a safe distance down the lane, we splashed some mud on the bumpers to cover the unit's numbers.

At camp, we headed straight for our mess equipment to find Sergeant Rother. We'd been friends for a long time and I knew that we could rely on him. He agreed to make the contraband vehicle disappear and quickly shuffled it in with his trucks.

This was not our first heist, nor would it be our last. I'm sure some considered us little better than thieves, but we fashioned ourselves more like Robin Hood.

Mess–Much More Than Met The Eye!

Paul Rother wore many hats throughout our time in Northern Europe. Although he served brief stints as a platoon sergeant and a first sergeant, I remember him most as our mess sergeant.

The position of mess sergeant entailed much more than you might imagine. They not only cared for the grub, but also for troubled psyches. At times, they were called on to corral a unit's worst. Although it may now seem insensitive, soldiers who experienced mental breakdowns while on the line were sometimes sent to the mess sergeant. Problems like "battle fatigue" and "shell shock" were very real, but difficult to discern. No one wanted to give a faker a free ticket home, so the most questionable cases were often moved to the mess area. The cooks kept a close eye on them for a few days or even a week. If the illness turned out to be legitimate, the suffering soldier was shipped to a hospital. If not, they went back to the front.

Sergeant Paul Rother
M Company, 358th Infantry

Within M Company, Sergeant Rother played a part in many delicate diagnoses. Although unschooled in medicine or psychology, he knew people. He was firm, but kind and possessed a disposition perfect for the task at hand. Given time, he could tell the difference between a scared boy and a sick man.

Mess was no free pass from combat either. When we needed them, they were there. More than once,

Sergeant Rother and his men were called to the front and thrown into the fray. He never disappointed.

Mortar Ammo Anyone?

Only days later, while on a recon patrol near Etain, we stumbled on a dozen, deserted German supply trucks. I'm not sure whether the drivers had been killed or captured. From the looks of it, maybe they'd had enough of this war and just left, AWOL. Much to our pleasure, we found two trucks, stacked to the brim with 80mm enemy mortar rounds. Although slightly smaller in size than our 81's, they still worked in our tubes.

We pulled the two Kraut trucks out of line, safely away and then disposed of the remainder. We shot holes in their gas tanks and set them ablaze. Ten burning trucks made for quite a fire.

On our way home, I set a couple of guys out on the hoods. I didn't want any GIs to mistake us for what we looked like, two German supply trucks. Without fail, we hit a convoy of American vehicles.

We approached cautiously, waved our hands and yelled, "Don't shoot! Don't shoot! We're Americans!" They thankfully received the message, loud and clear. A little more experienced at that sort of thing, they offered us reflective panels. When placed on hoods and truck tops, they were supposed to signal the Air Corps of our friendly nature.

Back at camp, Sergeant Rother couldn't spare any more men, so I tried our mortar platoon. When I showed them the two trucks, full of extra ammo, they were genuinely impressed. So much so, that they offered two drivers. All was well.

Love-Hate Relationship

While driving these enemy trucks, we not only worried about fire from ground units, but also from those up

above. Over time, we developed a real love-hate relationship with our boys in the sky. Let me first make clear
that we wildly applauded the vast majority for their courageous support of our efforts. On many occasions, they
seemed heaven sent to deliver us through the tightest of
squeezes. Most carefully identified targets before firing,
always at their own added risk. But, a select few didn't
bother. They were the ones that we hated. They shot at
anything that moved, friend or foe, and proved little less
than our worst enemy.

We complained through the proper channels, but nothing changed. With no alternatives, we decided to take
matters into our own hands and fire back, unofficially of
course. They just weren't getting the message any other
way. We felt that a few well-placed rounds carried more
weight than a written memo. The indiscriminate strafing
by the one or two loose cannons had to stop.

Not long thereafter, an Air Corps general visited our
camp. Before we started fighting back, the issue wasn't
worthy of their time. But now, they wanted to talk. Some
of our division brass tagged along. The controversy centered on a jeep driver, who after being hit one too many
times, returned fire from his mounted .50-caliber machine
gun. It sounded reasonable to me. Don't dish it out if you
can't take it! Apparently, he got their attention.

In defense, the driver provided any and all takers with
a tour of his vehicle. The evidence proved indisputable.
Although identification panels adorned the hood, fighter-
plane bullet holes decorated the frame.

After much deliberation, the high-priced jury concluded
that we all needed to be a little more careful. Wow, no
kidding? We'd been saying that for months! Most generals never ceased to amaze me, especially when in quo-
rum.

In the end, it wasn't words from the top, but rather, the
risk of retribution that solved the problem. I don't remem-

ber catching anymore friendly fighter-plane fire after that day.

Back To Work

We had vacated Chambois, well west of Paris, on August 22. In three weeks, we traveled through the bulk of northern France, some five hundred miles, with little to no resistance. We finally found and squared off with the enemy in the early morning hours of September 10, when the entire Battalion shoved its way into Fontoy, west of Thionville.

Although the unit histories will tell you otherwise, we weren't spoiling for a fight. We had all enjoyed the time off. It wasn't hard to get used to a life without flying metal.

Some were understandably apprehensive about heading back into battle. In Normandy, none of us believed we would survive, so we just went about our business as if on borrowed time. But after the one-sided victory at the Falaise Gap, followed by nineteen straight days of relative inaction, many had envisioned a life after this mess.

U. S. Army Signal Corps Photo, Courtesy National Archives

The 3rd Battalion, 358th Infantry takes
Fontoy, France - September 1944.

At Fontoy, where it was strictly a house-by-house encounter, we reacquainted ourselves with war. Mined road blocks and booby traps caused additional problems. Although our casualties were comparatively light, any American dead were significant. Far from welcome, the sounds and sites of battle had returned.

Hit Again!

The next day, we assaulted the hills surrounding the city of Algrange. It was always tough to expel an embedded enemy from good ground and this occasion proved no different. Well entrenched, they challenged each of our steps, hit us with everything they had—artillery, mortars, machine guns and small arms. But, we continued to force the issue. Several casualties soon dotted the tangled slopes.

While I worked up through some brush, an enemy round likewise ripped into me. The bullet pierced the meaty part of my inner left leg and exited just below my butt cheek. I knew immediately that I'd been shot, but was afraid to look. I felt pain in that whole area and initially feared the worst. When I finally mustered the courage to glance down, I was almost relieved to see blood flowing from a hole in my leg. I expanded the tear in my pants to witness the flesh peel away from the wound in layers, like when slicing a raw steak. I could stick a finger in both the "in" and "out."

I'd describe the bullet hole as "clean." Strictly a "meat wound," it severed no arteries or bones. On others, I'd seen larger, almost gaping holes. This was nothing like that. But, it still hurt like hell!

The stock on my M1 was shattered at nearly the same instance. Either separate bullets hit my gun and me or the same round first ricocheted off my weapon, then passed through my leg. Whichever the case, I believe the shell to have been well spent by the time it found its target—me.

I carefully rolled, crawled and scooted my way back down the hill. Once clear, I hobbled to our aid station. Multiple litters beat me there. My wound wasn't life threatening, so I grabbed a piece of dirt, grit my teeth, bore the pain and waited for my turn.

One of Doc Bulger's boys soon paid me visit. He probed both ends of the wound, filled each with sulfa powder, then wrapped a bandage around the entire leg. Under the circumstances, that's about all he could do.

Should I Stay Or Should I Go?

I privately debated my future. I didn't want to go back to the hospital. Cooped up with all those sad cases felt like slow torture to me. I hated that place! Since my initial visit, I vowed to avoid it at all costs.

My family was "M" and my home was at the front. But, could I physically carry on? Although I was in a lot of pain, my wound was through and through. No bullet remained in my body. No bones were broken. No arteries were cut. If I didn't need an operation, what could a hospital really do for me?

I spent that night at Doc's aid station. By morning, I could barely move. What I'd experienced the day before paled in comparison to my suffering at sunrise. It really tightened up on me.

Bulger stopped by to pamper an old friend. "If you can't move, you're going back!" he not so delicately advised, in true "Doc" fashion. He always said exactly what was on his mind, almost honest to a fault. Although his candid speech ruffled an occasional feather, it endeared him to many. Soldiers especially liked to hear it straight—the way it was. Doc fed it to them—the plain truth.

More reality than threat, his words lifted me to my feet. I limped around the immediate area. The leg was stiff, so

I kept it straight, much like a wooden peg or a broom handle. But after a time, it seemed manageable, especially when faced with the alternative. As the wounded began to truck west, I chose to stay.

Much Needed Time-Off

Just as quickly as we had reentered the combat, we again backed off. We spent two weeks in Division reserve at Sainte Marie Aux Chenes.[1] With all the drills, inspections and busy work, it reminded me of Camp Wolters, but I wasn't complaining. The break allowed me a much-needed head start on healing. I'm not sure I could have kept up without it.

When they said the word "showers," I almost lost my mind. I hadn't been clean since England. They trucked us to a designated area next to a small stream. Water was pumped from the creek through oil heaters, directly into the facilities. There was a small tent where you removed all your old moldy clothing; then came the showers. At least a hundred feet long, they ran the length of several tents tied together. A whistle sounded "all in," while only minutes later, another signaled "all out."

From there, we moved into a larger tent where we all received new clothing. There aren't words to describe how a clean body and a fresh set of clothes made me feel. I was a new man!

To and from the showers, we rode in 2.5-ton trucks. The mood was raucous on our way back. Everyone was so excited about the wash, rinse and new duds that we were really living it up. Then wham! Another truck and ours sideswiped each other. Normally it wouldn't have been that big a deal, but this time, arms hung over the railings. Many were mangled, some severely. I, luckily, sat on the other side. War was a dangerous place, even when not in battle.

*A new man! Sergeant Hobert Winebrenner after
a shower and new clothes - September 1944.*

Keep Drilling, Doc!

By venturing south to Mars la Tour, I also made use of
the reprieve to have a tooth filled. A dentist from Corps
Headquarters set up shop in the front room of an abandoned home. While he drilled out my decay, I admired a
nice little apple orchard across the way. Serving as the
energy source, his assistant pedaled away on what
looked like a stationary bike. Its revolutions turned a flex-
ible shaft that powered the drill.

While I sat in the chair and enjoyed the view out the front window, enemy artillery rounds began to fall about the neighborhood. Without any forward observers, the Germans were just stabbing in the dark, looking to get lucky or at least, do some collateral damage. A few shells landed across the street and uprooted several of the apple trees.

Not used to this part of the job, the dentist nervously looked at me and wondered aloud, "Maybe we should move down to the basement?"

By this time an expert on French housing, I assured him, "No basement in this home. Keep drilling, Doc!"

He cleaned her out and filled her up very well, considering the circumstances. The enemy artillery barrage chopped some wood, but did little else. I returned to camp and we moved out shortly thereafter.

Sergeant Hobert Winebrenner, all smiles at Mars la Tour - September 1944.

Gravelotte Duty

From Sainte Marie, we marched to Vionville. After two weeks off, my wound felt pretty good. I limped, but found staying active to be the best medicine. It not only kept my leg from stiffening, but it also kept my mind off the pain.

We set up another long-term camp. Now in on the siege of Metz, our Battalion drew the village of Gravelotte, just west of the fortress city. It served as our forward outpost. A single rifle company, with attached heavy machine-gun and mortar crews, manned the town at a time. Every few days, one combined unit rotated out, while another rolled in. When not on line, the remainder of the Battalion waited in reserve at Vionville. More time for healing!

On my group's first foray into Gravelotte, the weather accurately matched our mood as ominous clouds, low and black, hovered over our heads. With a column on each side of the road, we haggardly advanced toward impending doom. The rain fell in thick, heavy sheets. Step by step, we grudgingly slopped forward.

The Thunderbolts continued to fly, barely above the treetops. The ceiling couldn't have been more than a few hundred yards. Yet, they made regular runs to dive-bomb enemy targets. We all got the message. For them to work in that kind of weather, things must be bad up ahead. Metz must be a bear!

Although the Germans had vacated Gravelotte, they made their presence felt most every day. A string of enemy forts protected Metz from the west. Well within range, their big guns shelled us often. Fort Jeanne d' Arc was not only the closest, but also, one of the fiercest.[2] Much of Gravelotte lay in ruins as ruble littered her streets and alleyways. When not on patrol, we traded time between water-filled trenches and shelled-out buildings.

Recon was never riskier than west of Metz. So many

different American units crowded the same general area that a friendly fire catastrophe waited around each corner, behind every tree. We did our homework, carried on and hoped for the best. That's all we could do.

New meets old! Much of Fortress Metz dated back to the Middle Ages - October 1944.

Almost nightly, we received special assignments. Small groups were routinely ordered to tackle specific targets. More like guerilla warfare, we nibbled at the enemy's vast fortifications. Although objectives changed, the general plan did not—get in quick, do the damage and escape clean. Overtime, it all added up. We dealt a significant blow.

Troublesome pillboxes topped the list. Built like bomb shelters, these concrete bunkers were almost impenetrable to our weaponry. Their only weak spots lay in the slits and openings from which their occupants fired. We concentrated our collective metal on these points until we either killed the gunners or they shut the door. With the window sealed, we kept up the pressure while a demolition team worked forward with a satchel charge. Back in those days, a satchel charge amounted to no more than a bag full of explosives with a timer or remote detonating wire. The crew placed the sack on the sill, then scrambled for refuge. We kept up the cover fire so the Krauts wouldn't reopen the gap and chuck the charge back onto our own men. The blasts typically blew small openings into cave-size entrances. Those not killed by the explosion, surrendered without further resistance.

It may sound simple enough, but it wasn't. Keep in mind, while we're begging the Krauts to button up that hole, they're tearing through our ranks at a violent rate. They're surrounded by concrete, while we're hiding behind a tree or a mound of dirt. Taking out an enemy bunker took patience, perseverance, and more times than not, American casualties. Pillbox by pillbox, we battled the Maginot Line, west of Metz.

U. S. Army Signal Corps Photo, Courtesy National Archives

Typical enemy fortifications toeing the Maginot Line, barbed wire and pillboxes as far as the eye could see - October 1944.

*90th Division brass inspect a captured
Maginot Line bunker - October 1944.*

We spent the majority of October 1944 in and out of Gravelotte.[3] Beyond the frequent enemy barrages, I most remember the rain. More fell every day, and not just a sprinkle, but in buckets. Foxholes filled with water. Cold and wet, day and night, we were surely miserable. Although faced with an uncertain future, no one was sorry to leave Gravelotte duty behind.

Chapter 12

Into The Motherland

Cattenom, France to Butzdorf, Germany

Knitting The Night Away

In early November, we marched from Gravelotte to a staging area at the rear, where we honed our river-crossing skills. Practice makes perfect. We gradually worked our way north of Thionville to board in the forests west of Cattenom. No matter where we went, the rain followed.

1st Lieutenant Don Benedict rejoined our outfit. We were all surprised to see him. Few survived gunshot wounds to the face, let alone, returned to the front. But, there he was. As our senior officer, he took command of M Company.

With winter approaching, Supply issued us sleeping bags. Most of us didn't even bother with shelter halves anymore. We just got inside wherever we could. More times than not, we slept out in the open, under the stars. While on-line, we eked out an existence, lived more like stray dogs than human beings. But, such was life in war.

Along with the sleeping bags, we received two new blankets, a needle and some thread. "What's all this?" everyone's puzzled facial expression seemed to beg.

On closer inspection, the bags were just that—outside coverings with no insides. Unbelievable! Apparently unable to afford the extra nickel, our government expected us to sew in the liners. It served as a worthy example of how far removed the upper echelons were from life at the front. Although we both fought on the same side, we lived worlds apart.

With big ugly fingers, we knitted the night away like busy little worker bees, but no one cared much about the finished product. We put forth minimal effort, then piled the tangle. What a joke!

Our First River Crossing

The new month brought so much more than thundershowers. Little did we know then, the peril that awaited us. The *Regimental History, 358th Infantry* aptly summarized days ahead, *"... the month of November was to embrace one of the most memorable periods in the history of the 358th Infantry Regiment, and occupy a prominent place in the annals of American military operations."*[1]

At 1:00 a.m. on November 9, we got the call to move out.[2] Our Battalion would lead the attack across the Moselle River. On the other side, the German's Fort Koenigsmacker browbeat the entire region.

Days of continuous rain preceded our advance. Dirt roads resembled soup as we plunged ahead. Storm clouds stifled any hint of moonlight. The pitch-black night made it very hard to see, even a few feet in front of our faces. We inched forward to find our assault boats. My crew included our recently returned, 1st Sergeant Paul Inman and half a dozen others.

We sidled slowly toward the river in ankle-deep water, when a nearby explosion dropped us to the mud for cover. Caught in such an exposed position, we believed our minutes to be numbered. But then, no more fire. The blast turned out to be from one of our own grenades. We often fastened their handles to the webbing on our pack harnesses. Somehow a pin worked loose and detonated, while still attached to a GI's chest—not a pretty sight.

With each passing moment, the Moselle grew in speed and volume. The rain swelled her breadth. Decidedly more unruly, she began to overflow her banks at an alarming rate. What once seemed manageable, now appeared far from it.

U. S. Army Signal Corps Photo, Courtesy National Archives

90th Division infantrymen approach the mighty Moselle River - November 1944.

Sooner than planned, we set sail for the east coast. Inman manned the point, while I sat in back. Once out in the water, we spun in circles, around and around. Between the downpour and the darkness, it was difficult to discern why. Our vessel turned like a top as it rapidly swept downstream. I felt my way forward to discover that the guys on one side were paddling like crazy, while those on the other had hunkered down. Experienced seamen we were not.

I tapped the top of each cowering young man's helmet with the stock of my M1. Finally, they opened their eyes! We got her evened out and headed toward the opposite shore. But by then, we'd drifted way off course. We thankfully landed without incident and quickly rejoined our unit. All Inman and I could do was shake our heads and laugh. Maybe amphibious warfare wasn't our thing. The Marines need not worry about our team; their jobs were safe.

U. S. Army Signal Corps Photo, Courtesy National Archives

Row, row, row your plane? Afloat on the flooded Moselle River, a 90th Division crew attempts to paddle a stranded piper cub ashore - November 1944.

Like A Volcano!

Once beached, we were to roll around the north side of Fort Koenigsmacker. Ominous on the ridgeline, the Fort hovered over our shoulders like a bully spoiling for a fight.

Aside from the accidental grenade victim, Colonel Bealke numbered as our first casualty. Although not life-threatening, the wound was significant enough that he relinquished command, which was telling in that Bealke never shied from combat. Back across the river he went, replaced by Captain James Spivey.

We initially caught the Krauts napping and moved considerably inland before taking any fire. A cement factory topped our list of objectives. Thankfully, it wasn't heavily guarded and we secured it without delay. From there, things took a turn for the worse.

The Krauts awoke to angle their machine guns and cannons down the well-fortified knolls. Like a volcano, the hill erupted with enemy fire! American fighting men fell early and often.

Even though we weren't the unit directly assaulting Fort Koenigsmacker, we felt the brunt of her blows. In his *The Lorraine Campaign*, author Hugh M. Cole explained, *"Although the main case-mates housed a battery of four 100 mm guns, these could not be depressed to bear on the attacking 1st Battalion and during much of the subsequent fighting they continued to be fired on the 3rd Battalion as it worked its way forward in the draw to the north."* [3] In minutes, our number of casualties ballooned from two to dozens.

An anti-tank ditch sliced through the rolling terrain. As Lieutenant Mateyko approached, he noticed a handful of our most recent replacements standing straight up at its brim, casually admiring the view. Shocked by their naivete, he raced forward, hoping to herd them from harm's way. He launched himself at their small huddle in an attempt to bowl them over like pins at an alley, but an enemy artillery round hit at their feet. The blast careened upward to wound them all, some mortally. Apart from torn and tattered clothing, Mateyko was fine, spared yet again.[4]

The Germans stubbornly contested any and all movement, each and every one of our steps. Jerry threw immeasurable amounts of metal our way! Yet with nowhere to hide, we advanced forward. Amid heavy casualties, we slithered around the north side of Koenigsmacker to take up positions on a flanking ridgeline, Bois d' Elzange.

Long after the war, I took my daughter, Jane Ann, back to this place. Brush and briars consumed the area. In the distance, a combine calmly cut wheat from a field. We stomped around and tried to retrace my steps, but much had changed. The setting seemed tranquil, now at peace—a far cry from November 1944.

We Stood Alone

Bloated by steady rain, the Moselle resembled a lake more than a river, and a fast-moving one at that. Her waters were described as a "raging torrent."[5] Nothing moved either way across her ever-increasing breadth, now measuring a mile and a half.[6] All but the last house in Cattenom was flooded, while the main road lay under a foot of water.[7]

German artillery zeroed in on each bank and all spots between. Engineers couldn't complete pontoon bridges and sunken supply boats soon crowded the river bottom. Sadly, our precious sleeping bags numbered among the casualties. All that delicate sewing for naught! We never even got the chance to know them.

With all supply lines severed, the infantry stood alone. At 0940, on November 10, the 3rd Battalion log detailed our predicament. *"Our river problem is very acute. It's impossible to span anything across with the swelling that*

141

has come up and the swift current. The Bn is contacting everyone for aid but none seems to help. A last minute check reveals that we have nothing across; ammo, food or vehicles." [8]

There were no medical supplies, no blankets, but most of all, no armor. We faced fortified emplacements with only small arms—a daunting task!

U. S. Army Signal Corps Photo, Courtesy National Archives

In a race against the clock, 90th Division engineers work to bridge the swollen Moselle River - November 1944.

Once around Koenigsmacker, we inched our way south against fierce enemy resistance. Like two rams tied together, we butted heads by the hour. Because neither side could distance itself, the bludgeoning continued for days.

Although I didn't see him fall, K Company's Executive Officer, 1st Lieutenant Max Short was killed during this stretch. He was a man we worked with often—a good friend and a great officer. Everyone thought highly of him, none more so than "K's" Commanding Officer, Captain Robert McHolland.

K Company Command Team: Sedar, Rice, Short, McHolland

For extraordinary heroism, 1st Lieutenant Max Short earned the Distinguished Service Cross. The official citation read in part:

"... On 11 November 1944, the 358th Infantry met intense resistance during an attack against strong enemy positions near Koenigsmacker, France. Lieutenant Short, a platoon leader of Company "K" quickly reorganized his depleted platoon into an effective fighting force and daringly led them through intense fire in a bold assault. When the enemy retreated to prepared positions on the crest of a hill, Lieutenant Short and his men followed in pursuit and engaged them in a fierce hand-to-hand fight. Lieutenant Short killed one of the enemy with his gun butt and another with his trench knife before he fell, mortally wounded. Inspired by his heroic actions the platoon continued on and completely routed the enemy forces, killing and wounding many of them. ..." [9]

The *Regimental History, 358th Infantry* added, *"... Lt.*

Short issued orders that no man would fire until the enemy was within fifty yards—when his company was counter-attacked by a sizable enemy force. His orders were carried out to the last man and his men not only beat-off the counter-attack but accounted for the annihilation of most of the attacking force." [10]

Our easiest pickings lay in a sizable group of German reinforcements sent to bolster the besieged Fort. From concealed positions, we caught their columns on an open expanse and laid waste to almost the entire lot. Given the opportunity, and juiced by our own recent losses, we tore the enemy apart. At close range, our heavy machine guns cut them down by the dozens, if not by the hundreds. For a few moments, it felt like the Falaise Gap, but reality soon returned.

U. S. Army Signal Corps Photo, Courtesy National Archives

90th Division GIs look on at a line of enemy dead near Fort Koenigsmacker, France - November 1944.

In less than two days, our Battalion alone, suffered sixty-three casualties.[11] M Company friends and comrades, Harry Heavens, George Osborne, Ed Secord and Ted Zoch were all killed in the fighting.[12] The carnage was horrific, the suffering immense. Because of the monstrous Moselle, as the first snow of the season began to fall, we didn't even have blankets to cover our wounded. Yet despite our truly miserable circumstances, we pushed ever forward.

U. S. Army Signal Corps Photo, Courtesy National Archives

The 90th Division rolls through Koenigsmacker, France - November 1944.

The Self-inflicted

Shots from a barn interrupted the route march from Elzange to Inglange. We hurried to investigate.

Accompanied by a tall tale of a fleeing enemy force, two replacements sheepishly exited the structure. A crowd gathered to find one shot in the hand and the other, in the foot. Although this was a first for our unit, we all knew the score. Their wounds were obviously self-inflicted, a desperate attempt to get out of this godforsaken war and place.

1st Sergeant Paul Inman blew onto the scene like a vengeful storm. You've got to understand that 1st sergeants ruled the roost, kept soldiers and events in line for their captains. From the top to the bottom, they were the glue that held units together. Inman wore the role well.

M Company Photo by David Pond Willis

1st Sergeant Paul Inman
M Company, 358th Infantry

He cared deeply for his men, at least those who deserved it. Unfortunately for the two replacements, they did not. I'd never seen him that mad. He berated both for as long as his voice would allow. He ordered their platoon sergeants forward to rip the PFC stripes from their uniforms. When an aidman asked to bandage their wounds, Inman told him to stand clear. He wasn't yet finished. In closing, he promised to personally bring charges against each and testify at their trials.

Although no one said a word, we all inwardly applauded Inman's serious stand. We put our lives on the line daily. We had already lost how many brave men? If nothing else, Inman made clear that harming one's self would not be tolerated on his watch, would be no way out of his war. He was all a company could ask for in a 1st sergeant, and so much more.

We finally fought our way to Inglange and battled hard in and around the town. With the help of several newly arrived tankers, we secured the victory.

Low in both morale and men, we backed away for a few days off. We caught our collective breath in the town of Metzervisse; then recouped for a couple more days in Luttange.

U. S. Army Signal Corps Photo, Courtesy National Archives

A lone civilian weaves her way through lines of 90th Division infantrymen as they pass through war-torn Metzervisse, France - November 1944.

Into Germany

Sooner than later, trucks picked us up and motored us north into Germany. We unloaded near Perl. Now into the motherland, we all rightly assumed things would get worse before they got better. We set out for our next objectives, the towns of Tettingen and Butzdorf.

U. S. Army Signal Corps Photo, Courtesy National Archives

In two long columns, the 358th Infantry marches through the rain toward Tettingen and Butzdorf – November 1944.

I hated this area and this time in my life. We were wet all day, every day. By late November, the rain turned to ice and snow, and the wind howled, bitter cold. They say, "misery loves company" and we all felt it.

Anti-tank emplacements dominated the hills and valleys. The whole area was terribly tough on armor. Those pieces fortunate enough to survive the surging Moselle met one obstacle after another. Nothing came easy. Any headway was hard earned. Consequently, we often fought alone.

U. S. Army Signal Corps Photo, Courtesy National Archives

*Barbed wire and dragon's teeth marked the
Siegfried Line for miles – November 1944.*

Not long into our journey, we hit a sizable tank trap. They amounted to little more than large ditches, undoubtedly dug by slave labor. But once down in these things, tanks either couldn't get out because of the steep opposite banks or if they did, the extreme upward angle exposed their vulnerable underbellies to enemy fire— hence the term "tank trap."

Weeks of rain had filled this particular one full. With winter upon us, the standing water froze into ice. Our first few men poured in with high hopes to skate across the thin layer. Their dreams were shattered with the ice. They broke through to plunge into a pool of waist-deep slush. We then tried to get cute and bridge the gap with ladders, but we lacked time and patience. In the end, we all just skidded down into the frigid abyss, waded across

149

and climbed up the other side. What a miserable feeling! Wet and icy cold, our clothes froze about our bodies in minutes.

We fled the trap into a dense forest, where a waiting enemy pinned us down. The woods were so thick and the fire so intense that our units lost track of each other. As in Normandy, the fighting deteriorated into squad or pocket warfare.

I dug in with a heavy caliber machine gun and crew. We dealt a lot of damage, but also suffered a significant amount in return. Although I didn't get hit, several within my group did. That night, the Germans threw artillery rounds in on us for good measure. Wet clothes, frigid temperatures, torrential enemy fire—things couldn't get worse. Or, could they?

The next morning, we finally freed ourselves from the woods. Pillboxes surrounded Butzdorf to force confrontations, one position at a time. Still far from our objective, we'd already lost countless men along the way.

A Bad Day At Butzdorf

We paused briefly on a ridge overlooking the village. I was in a group of machine gunners attached to K Company, now commanded by our old friend and former mate, Captain Robert McHolland. Past heroics had not only earned him charge of "K" and a promotion to the rank of captain, but also two Silver Stars. Known as the "Kraut Killers," his rifle unit numbered among the best in the business of war. They had become almost legendary for their courage under fire—a true reflection of their CO.

For his combined efforts the day before and earlier that morning, McHolland received the Distinguished Service Cross. The official citation read in part:

" ... *On 23 November 1944, during an attack by the 358th Infantry against strongly fortified enemy positions*

near Tettingen, Germany, Captain McHolland, command-
ing Company "K" fearlessly led a group of his men
against a concrete machine-gun emplacement,
destroyed it with a demolition charge and forced the
occupants to surrender. The following day he again dis-
tinguished himself by breaking up a strong enemy attack
against his command post. When the enemy force
retreated, Captain McHolland and two enlisted men bold-
ly pursued them, killed fourteen of the attackers with
hand grenade fire, wounded seven and forced the
remaining seventy-eight to surrender. ..." [13]

90th Division Commander, General James Van Fleet
awards Captain Robert McHolland with the Silver Star.

As we set our sights on Butzdorf, Company I was
assigned to Tettingen and "L" waited in reserve.[14] By this
stage, we had lost all radio contact, with anyone—period.
We were truly in it alone. But with no red flags from intelligence, we assumed our objective to be manageable.

First, we had to traverse a wide-open valley into the village. Rather than rumble forward en masse, we trickled
into town, a few guys at a time. It was a shrewd move by

McHolland and most of us made it safely into three or four of the outlying houses.

Structure by structure, we began to fight our way through Butzdorf. Our biggest problem lay in our heavy machine guns. I think only parts of two made it, and neither worked worth a damn. Outside the village, we had waded through yet another deep, slush-filled anti-tank ditch. Our guns got wet. Even though we dismantled, cleaned and dried them, they never again lived up to expectations.

That night, German reinforcements trotted into town, and began to push us back. We soon worked from only a handful of houses at the village's outer edge. However, these structures happened to occupy both sides of the main road running from Butzdorf to Tettingen.

When a German rifle company came marching down this avenue, seemingly unaware of our presence, we couldn't help but lick our chops. We hoped to catch them between us, in a crushing crossfire. But unfortunately, the plan never materialized. One overly eager sergeant failed to contain his energy. Just as the enemy columns pulled even, he leapt out onto the porch to cut them down with a Thompson submachine gun. It was way too soon! He hit several before his weapon jammed. But in losing the element of surprise, we'd fumbled away our one and only advantage.

With no choice but to join him, we poured round after round into the exposed enemy—tossed grenades by the dozens. But there were too many, and the rear portions of their lines hadn't even made it into town yet. The survivors quickly found cover, returned fire and joined the siege.

A very bad situation turned even worse when two Kraut tanks arrived, and they weren't shy about deconstruction. The enemy armor dismantled one building after another. We were left with only three houses.

With no radio, we would have to escape to find help. Members of my house tried several times, but to no avail. Enemy fire slammed our doors shut! I'm sure the other groups attempted to flee as well, with similar results. The only thing we really had going for us was the darkness, which always made things a little more difficult.

Fellow M Company trooper, Sergeant Howard Pemberton was holed up in a house with Captain McHolland and maybe a dozen others. I remember their home well. It was larger than ours, on the same side of the road, but closer to Tettingen. They too had their eyes set on escape. "It was decided that I was going to go get help," Pemberton later explained. "I was just getting ready to leave. Captain McHolland was the doorman. Then we heard a guy trying to yell quietly, but still be heard, 'K! K! K! K Company!' as he ran alongside the shed toward the door. When McHolland opened it to let this guy in, an enemy machine gunner cut the Captain down, right in front of me. There was nothing we could do for him. McHolland was dead and I never made it out the door." [15]

Sergeant Howard Pemberton
M Company, 358th Infantry

We not only had no contact with the outside world, but also, very limited communications with one another. No one beyond that house knew Captain McHolland had been killed. In many ways, each individual structure— each separate band of soldiers, stood alone.

At one critical point during that very long night, the Krauts concentrated their collective efforts on the house across the way from us. They were trying to literally flatten it! The German panzerfausts and tanks blew holes clean through. It was dark! We were firing! They were firing! Explosions everywhere! What a confused mess! But in the end, the house came down.

Several fleeing friends actually made it safely to our structure. I have no idea how, but I remember it happening. More still, never made it out alive.

The tremendous commotion served as a worthy distraction, which allowed another and myself to escape. Riflemen from "K" screened our break as we pinched out the back, through the enemy lines. We first crawled away from Butzdorf, then ran for the woods outside Tettingen. We had to find help!

Meanwhile, back in the village, Pemberton's gang continued to hold their own. "Two Germans came in through the shed and started yelling, 'Handy ho! Handy ho!'" he recounted. "No one answered them, so they got scared and headed back out. One of our boys cut them down before they made it. ... We got a hold of a German machine gun and started firing it. I think some of the other Krauts recognized the sound and thought we were with them. That might be the only reason why we made it through the night and next morning." [16]

My partner and I sprinted frantically, but by the time we reached help, our closest comrades in Company I were already actively engaged in Tettingen. Instead, Company L drew the assignment. A task force with attached tankers rolled toward Butzdorf. [17]

Those still trapped inside were now on their last legs. "We noticed a huge number of Germans forming three or four blocks away," Pemberton continued. "We could actually see an officer looking at us through field glasses. One of the guys asked me, 'Well, what are we going to do now?'

"I said, 'We might as well fight.' And that's just what we did. We opened up on them with everything we had. When they recovered to return fire, we had to get in the hallway. They were just blowing that house apart!

"A little later, I climbed up in the belfry and noticed tanks up on the hill. I thought, 'That's it! We're finished!' But when I looked again, I noticed the stars on their sides. They were American tanks! Battalion came in, took the town and saved us!"[18]

A Family Mourns

Sergeant Howard Pemberton earned a Silver Star for his heroics at Butzdorf. But the medal meant little to him, in light of McHolland's death. "We had been close friends from the time he joined M Company," Pemberton related. "The night before we went to Butzdorf, we walked through the woods together. ... I could see the fatigue in his eyes. I tried to get him to go back for a rest, but I knew he would never do it. ... He was one of the finest people I ever met."[19]

I didn't find out about Captain McHolland's death until much later that night. It may have even been Pemberton who told me, but I can't recall. I wasn't shocked because I'd been in Butzdorf and knew how bad it was. "M" machine gunners, Phil Dodds, Ed Hovencamp and George Maxwell died too that day, not to mention all of our wounded.[20] But, it still hurt to hear about "Mac." He was a friend to all.

On Saturday, November 25, 1944, the *Regimental History, 358th Infantry* made special mention of a hero gone, but never forgotten.

"On this night, the Regiment mourned the loss of a brilliant officer. Captain McHolland, who came overseas with the Regiment, had formed his company in the heavily shelled woods of the Foret de Mont Castre—out of a handful of replacements and a few old members of the company. From that time on, he became one of the most outstanding commanders in the Regiment—instilling in the men the finest qualities of a soldier. If there was a tough job to be done K Company took it and liked it. The story of Captain McHolland already had become a legend and his name will long be remembered by every man who knew of him." [21]

None felt the loss more than his family. "I was only three years old, but I remember Robert," beamed his nephew, Jerry Wiley. "On what was apparently his last leave … I recall him taking my younger brother, Bob, and me somewhere to get candy and ice cream. I also recall being at our home in Hurley one night and him teasing and scaring us with his stories about the bears and lions outside the windows. … He delighted in teasing everyone he knew.

"The most vivid early memory I have, and probably the one that has most affected my life, is the day in December 1944 when my mother received the telegram informing her that Robert was missing in action. The specific thing I remember is her calling her half-sister, Anna Hill, in Texas to tell her of the news. I remember her trying to talk through the sobs and tears on the old wall telephone we had in our home. I was very young, but I knew something was very wrong because my mother couldn't stop crying." [22]

In a December 1945 ceremony at Springfield's O'Reilly General Hospital, Brigadier General George B. Foster presented three of Captain McHolland's nephews with his combat medals. Tom Hill received Robert's Distinguished Service Cross; Jerry Wiley received his Silver Star with Oak Leaf Cluster and Bob Wiley received his Bronze Star. [23]

"Uncle Bob was my hero, all the while I was growing up," Jerry added. "Many times I poured over the scrapbook my mother and aunt kept with clippings, pictures, and letters from and about him. ... Over the years, I came to know how much his family and friends thought of him. I guess, maybe, that's why he became, in absentia, my role model. I chose Army ROTC and served in the Infantry and wore his Infantry 'crossed rifles' insignia and Captain's bars when I was on active duty." [24]

A Man To Remember

Shortly after his death, a very dear friend of Robert's, Mary Scott Hair wrote a moving tribute entitled, "Rosary For Remembrance." In fact, the piece was so noteworthy that Missouri Congressman, Dewey Short had it entered into the May 21, 1946, *Congressional Record.*

Beyond her own insights, Hair's heartfelt remarks contain excerpts from some of Robert's letters home. A June 26, 1944, correspondence from France proves particularly revealing. It touched on his selfless reasons for fighting, hopes for future generations and undying optimism. Robert wrote:

"I am enclosing some pictures I found on the battlefield. I did not take them from a dead German—the Krauts carry pictures of their loved ones, too. Any personal belongings such as letters and pictures are scattered like leaves, after a battle.

"I studied these pictures carefully. This one of the little boy and his mother—there will be no swastikas for him. He will have a chance to grow up in a free world where

he can think for himself, a free man.

"Not only for Jerry, Bobby, Johnny, and Thomas Earl (McHolland's nephews), but for any children and for all people everywhere, will our sacrifices be made—that they may live the 'Abundant Life' due them.

"I firmly believe that peace will triumph over war and that love will rule the world." [25]

*Captain Robert McHolland
K Company, 358th Infantry,
KIA – November 24, 1944 Butzdorf, Germany*

McHolland was an ardent Christian, strong in his faith. In one of his last letters home, on October 15, he wrote from France:

"Today is Sunday. If the situation is favorable we may have some kind of service this afternoon.

"I am sending you a pressed flower. I found it in a German officer's medical manual.

"If the Lord is willing, I'll be seeing you all, some day." [26]

In closing, Hair eloquently offered the following thoughts, in remembrance of her fallen friend.

" ... The words from the beautiful song, 'The Rosary,' come to mind again and again—'O memories that bless and burn—O barren gain, and bitter loss—' That a life so young and so promising should be sacrificed seems, at times, 'A bitter loss.'

"But there was One who died on the Cross of Calvary, that men might live triumphant lives. And the words come again—in the whisper of wind in the leaves, in the voices of happy children at play, in the peace and quiet of the early morning—'Greater love hath no man than this, that a man lay down his life for his friends." [27]

We'd Be Back!

The 10th Armored soon relieved us. We staggered back into France. In his, *Battle History of the 3rd Battalion, 358th Infantry,* Lt. Colonel Charles B. Bryan numbered our losses. *"During the 'Tettingen Incident' the Battalion suffered as casualties seven officers and at least 148 men. ..."* [28]

A History of the 90th Division in World War II aptly described our well-being, or lack thereof. *"At the end of three days, enemy action and trench foot had reduced the effective rifle strength of one battalion to a mere 100. The serious drain in the Regiment's strength, plus the grueling period of action it had seen during the preceding two weeks were more than sufficient reasons to effect immediate relief of the exhausted 358th. ..."* [29]

The Germans had greeted us less than warmly on our initial foray into their country. In less than three weeks of fighting, our Regiment alone lost 140 men killed, 721 wounded and 59 missing.[30] Instead of a hardy handshake, we got a boot to the face. But, we'd be back!

Chapter 13

Rebel Soldier Or One-eyed Ass

Saar River to Dillingen, Germany

The Mighty Saar

The weather worsened as December brought more cold accompanied by occasional flurries. Yet, the war stopped for nothing, even winter. After a brief break, where we licked our wounds and received far too few replacements, we again hit the road. This time, instead of north, supply trucks hauled us east to the German border. From drop-off to destination, we marched for hours through dirt and darkness to the town of Oberlimberg. The next day, officers prepared us for our second river crossing. The mighty Saar now lay in our path.

On the early morning hours of December 6, we set out.[1] After several more miles of mud, we paused atop a very tall bluff, overlooking the river. I was shocked to learn that this was where we'd cross her swift currents. Strategy most certainly picked that point. Neither we, nor our enemy would have suspected as much. It offered that ever-elusive, always coveted element of surprise.

After negotiating the steep descent to the bank below, our forces spanned the swollen Saar without incident. Germany sat silent as we forged ahead, en masse.

U. S. Army Signal Corps Photo, Courtesy National Archives

A 90th Division mortar crew, firing high explosive (HE) rounds, softens fortified German positions along the Saar River – December 1944.

Pressed To The Floor

A tremendously flat, wide-open meadow ran from the river's east edge to the tiny town of Pachten, our initial objective. As our forward units eyed her outskirts, the entire area awoke. Several pillboxes along the way, bypassed by earlier units, now erupted. Concrete block bunkers, disguised as houses, came to life. German artillery pounded the crossing.

Enemy machine gunners, safe in their shelters, pinned my section of the caravan to the ground. Flat on our faces, we dug and clawed at the dirt in a desperate attempt to form any kind of barrier between our helmets and the incoming shells. There wasn't time for entrenching tools. Each soldier pushed mud and scooped sod with his bare hands. Before long, I'd shelved my body slightly below bullet level.

Literally with us only a few days, some of our newest replacements were understandably overwhelmed. Near my position, one young man, without thinking, simply sat up to ask for direction. I watched in horror as multiple machine-gun rounds struck him about the face and upper torso. The velocity of the blasts slammed him violently back to the surface. Half his head was gone, but I didn't call for help. Medics couldn't fix puddles of gray matter. I didn't know his name or anything about him. Sometimes it hurt less that way.

Some within our gang found refuge in an anti-tank ditch. Sergeant Howard Pemberton numbered among this fortunate few. Yet again, instead of hunkering down, he took to the offensive. "Earlier that day, we had a guy chicken-out—decided all of a sudden that a little scratch was worthy of the aid station," Pemberton explained. "He dropped his bazooka and left. We had ammo, so I just picked it up and carried it with me. ...

"...Across the river, those German machine gunners were kicking up dirt all over the place. But sometimes, they rattled those things so fast that they jammed. When I heard that gun pause, I stood up with the bazooka on my shoulder. The pillbox was about fifty yards away and the slit was maybe only a foot wide by eight inches high. I fired that thing and the round went right into that opening. It ricocheted around in there for what seemed like forever and killed them all." [2] For that feat, Pemberton earned his second Silver Star in less than two weeks.

*90th Division Commander, General James Van Fleet pins
a second Silver Star on Sergeant Howard Pemberton.*

Search For Support

The enemy bullets buzzed overhead like bees. In response, our artillery banged back, but their shells were landing far too deep. We needed support along the town's edge, not beyond. Initially, their well-intentioned efforts offered little tangible assistance.

As was often the case, our radios were out and we had no spotter. Experienced both in artillery and recon, I soon received orders to manually relay a message back to the big guns, to adjust their fire. Just one cannon and a few good hits would get us into town.

I corralled another less than eager participant to join me, in case I didn't make it. "Getting up" ranked as one of the hardest requests I've ever made on my body. Only moments before, with eyes wide-open, I'd witnessed a kid take several in the head. Now I would be the one up, running around? After a heated war within, I raised just enough to scamper toward the river. My partner followed.

Thankfully, the German gunners either didn't notice us or had found success somewhere else along the line. By the time their fire chased after us, it was too late. We had made it safely to the Saar.

Beyond the enemy pillboxes, long-range Kraut cannons continued to hammer the crossing. The initial stages of a span sat dormant. Amid the chaos, engineers could only watch and wait for a lull in the action. Several from Supply crowded the would-be bridgehead, but they weren't the people I needed. They couldn't help me.

U. S. Army Signal Corps Photo, Courtesy National Archives

90th Division combat engineers work to span the Saar River with a pontoon bridge – December 1944.

The two of us hopped into an empty assault boat and paddled across. Like the Moselle, the Saar had escaped its banks. Swift and swollen, she swept us well downstream. Once deposited on the opposite shore, we retraced our earlier steps. In time, we happened on a handful of cannons. Forward, but not actively engaged, the small crew warmed themselves around four or five fires. Rather than look for a group already on line, we tried our luck with these guys. The two of us marched to the closest gathering and presented ourselves to a sitting sergeant.

Chin deep into a canteen cup of coffee, he swiveled his head to ask, "What can I do for you?"

"We need some help!" I quickly answered, then briefed him on our situation. With over a year at Fort Sill, I spoke his language.

When he continued to casually slurp on, I fully expected some kind of wishy-washy response. But instead, he finished his drink, looked me square in the eyes and offered, "Lead the way! I'm in!"

He must have worked in Transportation because he immediately put the wheels in motion. Not once did he fret about permission from superiors. He just got the job done. Within a matter of minutes, he assembled a cannon crew and a truck caravan. A track vehicle led the way and pulled the howitzer. A supply truck followed, loaded with artillery ammo. A small bulldozer brought up the rear.

Through field glasses, I pointed out prospective targets, while they set up the cannon, back from the bluff. But like the other pieces, it also lobbed rounds too deep. The barrel wouldn't depress far enough. We were either too close or too high. I was a little concerned, but the sergeant took it all in stride. He called in the dozer to push some dirt away, which allowed the cannon's front end to drop down deeper. The next group of shells hit dead-on perfect, just what we needed! As our newfound friend softened enemy positions, we re-crossed the Saar and returned to the battle.

We Meet Again

In the late 1960s, my wife, Marian and I traveled by train from Fort Wayne, Indiana, to Omaha, Nebraska, for the annual 90th Division Reunion. We unloaded at the old Omaha Train Station and took a cab to the Castle Hotel.

After check-in, we wandered toward the restaurant in search of breakfast. On our way, we passed a familiar-looking man, but I couldn't quite place him. When I turned for another glance, I noticed that he did the same. We walked to each other and questioned in unison, "Where in the hell do I know you from?"

We soon straightened it all out. His name was Carl Manuel and he hailed from Fort Smith, Arkansas. He was the one, the artillery transportation sergeant who had helped us, outside Pachten, Germany. Back on that day, I neglected to even get his name, but after Omaha, I'd never forget it. Carl joined Marian and me for breakfast— pan-fried mush, soft-fried eggs, good coffee and great conversation. Although we hadn't met but once in our lives, we reminisced like long-lost friends.

I've always realized that he went out on a tremendous limb for us and could have faced dire consequences as a result. For all those years, from December 1944 to our meeting that day, a single question nagged at me. Why—why had he helped us? Finally given the opportunity, I just threw it out.

In silence, he gathered himself and his answer. Oddly enough, the story revolved around an ancestor of his, a Confederate soldier. When the guy was discharged at the end of the Civil War, the Yankees allowed him a mule—a one-eyed one at that. From Alabama, he walked back home to Arkansas. Barefoot, broke and at the helm of this visually challenged ass, he must have proved quite a sight for all to see. He ambled through parts of multiple states before finally hitting home. All along the way, kindly strangers took him in, fed and cared for him.

"That's about how I felt for you two that night at the Saar River," Carl admitted. "You were two of the sorriest looking soldiers I'd ever seen."

Sergeant Carl Manuel and his wife, Lorena – 1942.

Now that I think about it, our appearance had seen better days. Covered brown from head to toe, we had spent the last several hours face down in fresh mud.

"Truth be known, you reminded me of the story about my grandpappy and his one-eyed mule," he continued. "Folks took him in, so I did the same for you—no more, no less." I was curious to know which I most resembled, the rebel soldier or the one-eyed ass, but chose not to ask for fear of the answer.

Silver Star

Beyond Pachten sat its much larger and far more evil sister city, Dillingen. That place was full of Krauts! We initially fought on and around a large rail yard, where crews connected and dismantled trains. Many sets of tracks, numerous cars and lots of German soldiers cluttered the neighborhood.

The battle pitched into a real tug-of-war at this depot—push and pull, hour after hour, with heavy losses on both sides. Although we momentarily rumbled ahead into the city and repelled multiple counterattacks, we were eventually saddled with more than we could handle. A surging Kraut mob forced us back several structures. Disengaging the enemy while under heavy fire was tenuous at best, deadly at worst, and this time proved no different. House by house, we attempted to distance ourselves, but we suffered significant casualties in the process. Ultimately, there came to be too many, too close to our position. Essentially trapped, my small group circled the wagons, buttoned up a rag-tag perimeter and readied for the end.

As if things weren't bad enough already, I noticed an enormous number of legs assembling on the other side of the parked train cars, hundreds of them. Add scores of Germans to the already uneven mix and we were finished—checkmate. The word "overran" came to mind.

We had to find some mortar or artillery support, but lacked the means to get it. I knew what needed to be done, but instead of a radio or a phone, I had a machine gun. Only minutes away from annihilation, I had to act.

The official citation for my Silver Star described the events. It read:

"For gallantry in action on 15 December 1944 in the vicinity of Dillingen, Germany. During a counterattack, Sergeant Winebrenner attempted to direct mortar fire upon the enemy but found that all of his means of communication had been knocked out. Remembering where a mortar observer had previously hidden a radio from the enemy, he, at risk of his life, crossed open terrain under heavy fire to find the radio still intact in its hiding place. Ignoring the intense fire, he returned over the same hazardous route to a position from which he could observe the enemy. He then set up his radio and, by directing accurate mortar fire on the attackers, repelled the counterattack and inflicted heavy casualties upon the enemy. His gallantry was in accordance with high military tradition." [3]

I caught a ton of enemy machine-gun fire out in no man's land. I heard the bullets snap, buzz and ricochet all around me, but I never got hit. God was surely with me that day.

I made it back to my position just as the mass of Germans rounded the end of the cars and began their charge toward us. Amazingly, the radio still worked and I didn't waste a second in calling our mortar platoon. I had no time for locating rounds. Jerry was nearly on us! I shouted what I believed to be the correct coordinates and called for effect. Our mortar men let go with all they had, round after round of HE and WP. The close-in fire fell like rain, directly on the advancing enemy. Those Krauts never knew what hit them. Shells exploded everywhere and tore the enemy soldiers to bits. We gladly jumped on our MGs and added to the storm.

More than me, our mortar platoon smashed the counterattack. In no way could the barrage have been more on time or on target. They deserve the credit.

It was such an intense experience that for decades I relived it in my dreams. In deep sleep, I returned to war. From the bedroom to the battlefield, as if back in Dillingen, I screamed coordinates, begged for our mortar men to throw down that fire, and fast. My wife Marian endured years of my heated, middle-of-the-night cries. Initially, it frightened her, but over time, she grew to accept it as part of who I am. Thankfully, I've now laid it to rest. At least, that's what she tells me.

House By House

We rebounded back into the first few blocks beyond the railroad tracks. Steadily, we crept along—room by room, house by house, street by street, sunup to sundown. On better days, we secured several city blocks. While on others, furious counterattacks erased all previous gains. It shaped up as one hell of a bloody urban brawl, perhaps the worst we'd ever experienced. We got so low on men that they pushed the supply guys, cooks and MPs into service on the front lines.

With a depleted machine-gun section, I jumped into a memorable house that began where a street ended, at a T-intersection. From the front to the back, a hallway stretched straight in line with this avenue. We didn't think much of it, until the enemy rounds followed us home. With a beautiful field of fire from a building down the way, a German gun crew launched slugs directly into the entryway. With both doors open, some shells actually passed cleanly through and didn't hit a thing. The outer rooms and walls knocked many others down. We stayed toward the back, returned fire when able, and crossed the exposed corridor only sparingly.

Yet, in the midst of this gun battle, our enemy must have switched types of ammo, for nothing stopped their bullets now! They traveled all the way through the walls, rooms and house with minimal effort. The change immediately commanded attention.

"Everybody out!" I screamed, amid an equal mix of exploding building materials. We hurriedly vacated the premises and moved on down the line in search of more suitable accommodations.

And that wasn't the exception, but rather, the rule. I'd never had so many houses literally torn apart around me in all my life. There was nothing quite like Dillingen.

Unlikely Feast

One night stands out, not for its violence, but for its unlikely feast. As evening approached, we scavenged for food. A number of backyards maintained pens, which housed tender young rabbits. We gathered a bushel basket full, maybe a dozen to feed our small group. We cleaned and dressed them, ready to cook. The meal promised to be special.

Barns accompanied most homes. Some were attached, while others sat apart, in the rear. I discovered a milk cow in one. Fresh milk rated as such a rare commodity that I had to give it a try. As I tugged on the cow's tits, flak from artillery shells intermittently pelted the structure. They were short rounds from one of our own units. By then, it was dark and a single candle provided only limited lighting. Every time metal hit that rooftop, the cow jumped, the candle shook and the flame flickered. Shadows danced wildly about the walls.

After a great deal of effort and a few close calls, I scored one cup of milk. Wow! I strained it and returned to the Dillingen dinner party to proudly sport my trophy.

We divided it into small portions, really just whistle-wetters. But oh, what a feeling!

Most cellars contained canned fruit and assorted other goodies. We also scrounged up some potatoes and bread. For the table arrangement, we borrowed nice china and silverware. Quite honestly, we spared no expense. Near show time, we brightly lit the room with an abundance of candles.

As we laid out this meal fit for kings, Lieutenant Mateyko haggardly shuffled in. He'd just finished setting perimeter defenses and graciously accepted our invitation to dinner. He seemed a bit overwhelmed by such a beautiful sight, tucked deep in this brutal realm. We almost forgot about the war for awhile.

Lessons Learned

That night into the next several days, the scene stabilized considerably. We actually made headway. The wild enemy counterattacks ceased to exist, replaced instead, by more manageable resistance.

Sergeant Allan McInnis, already two Purple Hearts heavier and only recently returned from an English hospital, fought for Dillingen's center. He and his battled-hardened machine-gun section liberated city hall. After lowering the high-flying Nazi flag, he had his boys autograph it. The banner remains with him, yet today.[4]

We caught wind that there was an enormous slaughterhouse, open for business in our sector of the city. While on an ammo and water run, several of us stopped by to have a look. Dressed pork halves and huge quarters of beef packed the cooling room. Fresh meat was always on the grocery list, so we helped ourselves to all we could carry. You couldn't look in any direction without seeing a dirty GI with half a pig or quarter of a cow slung over his shoulder. As bad as Dillingen was, we never ate better.

Also low on sources of light, we grabbed a fair amount of candles from a local church. Some were unmistakably ceremonial, quite large and adorned with ornamental crosses. But at the time, we didn't think twice and lit them that night.

When Lieutenant Mateyko stopped by while making his rounds, he went through the roof. I'd never seen him like that. He lectured us about the sanctity of certain items and demanded that we extinguish the candles and return them to the church at dawn.

We knew Mateyko was a religious man, but a well–oiled evangelist he was not. In fact, busy with the war, he rarely talked about it. I guess, rather than self-righteous rhetoric, he let his actions speak for his faith. In retrospect, they offered a much more convincing testimony.

I admired Mateyko for his strength of character and respected him for sticking to his convictions. We all learned a valuable lesson that night, not only on what was holy, but also about our leader.

Our leader, John Mateyko
M Company, 358th Infantry

Thank God For Cellars!

By two weeks in, we had sectioned and secured the vast majority of the city. Only the outlying reaches still lay in enemy hands. Dillingen was ours.

Even so, our cannons continued to hammer German positions. Without pause, they'd been at it for the entirety of the encounter. We wondered where they got all the shells.

Back in World War II, artillery was far from an exact science. We spent one of our last nights in Dillingen holed up in the basement of a two-story brick building. By morning, the upper levels were gone. What a night! Thank God for cellars!

But in tight squeezes, the barrages had to be close in to be effective. If you didn't feel the heat, the targeted enemy across the street probably didn't either. We accepted the risk in hope that the benefit would exceed the cost. Although it took a while to dig out of the debris the following morning, there sure weren't any Krauts around.

A Change In Plans

We all fully expected to mop up the remaining German resistance, then move out of Dillingen and onto the next adventure, but it never happened. Instead, we strangely stayed put and soon received the always-welcome mail call. I was elated to get two boxes from home, one from Mom and the other from my Aunt Lucinda. They both contained angel food cakes, packaged in popcorn. I quickly became the most popular guy in town. I rationed the popcorn among the masses, but kept the cakes for myself.

We found a partially intact home to pass a few hours away. I lounged on a bed to enjoy my desserts, but a runner banged the door open to announce, "We're backing out of Dillingen, tonight!"

"What the hell?" we all questioned. We had earned the town in a raw, bare-knuckled brawl. American dead stained the city's streets and alleyways blood red. And now, we were leaving like it had all been a bad dream? Dillingen was ours and now, we were handing it back to the Germans? What of the sacrifice? Was it all in vain?

The Lorraine Campaign tallied our unit's grim losses at Dillingen. *" ... the 90th Division ... had suffered severely, particularly among its veteran officers and men, and had lost 239 killed, 924 wounded, approximately 440 missing, as well as over a thousand officers and men evacuated as sick, battle-exhaustion, or battle-injury cases, the whole totaling more than one-third of its strength on 1 December."* [5]

Although none of us were happy about it, we didn't ask questions. We knew better by then. I put what was left of the two cakes into a pillowcase and tied them around the barrel of my gun—hobo style. As I strode out the front door and past the picket fence, enemy 88 rounds continued to rain upon the city.

At the river's edge, we paused to regroup. The plan was to pull out, company by company, platoon by platoon. My unit sat somewhere in the middle. Many had already crossed ahead of us, while rear guards continued to trade fire in town. Support outfits had worked day and night over the past week to span the Saar with supplies. But now, we had no time to use them, nor any way to get them back across. We burned much, rather than allow it to our enemy.

A shadowy outline of men disappeared into the darkness. Single file, they sidled to the Saar. Closer still, I noticed a white line trailing over the water. It was luminous tape secured to a floating footbridge. "Oh, no!" I winced at the sight. What our engineers labeled a "foot-bridge," I called a living nightmare. A fiery descent straight to hell would be less intimidating. A tenuous mix of cork slabs and aluminum channel, it danced to many different tunes. And in the darkness, you couldn't actually see it. Only the luminous tape led the way.

Our spacing had to be perfect. Too much weight in one area caused the structure to sink. Keep in mind that a normally large Saar River had swelled well beyond her banks, with an even swifter moving current. After one look at the bridge, most of us longed to be back in Dillingen, trading bullets with the Krauts.

Unavoidably, my turn arrived. We tried to keep some distance, maybe a ten-foot interval between us. But, the enemy artillery rounds wreaked havoc. When one landed on the opposite shore, the guys in front froze. We began to bunch up, out in the middle. Before long, we stood knee-deep in rolling water, panic-stricken, sinking fast, only seconds from total disaster. But, we couldn't quit! If we stopped, we all might as well have just jumped in. We had to plug away at a steady pace and trust one another to do the same.

Finally, the guys up front got it going again. We evened her out and eventually made it across. But, let's just say that the river wasn't the only thing getting my pants wet. As scary as combat, that experience will never be forgotten.

What's Next?

Back into France, we waited for new orders. It was a time of quiet reflection. Some of us were still steamed over our abandonment of Dillingen. Yet, we weren't privy to all the information. We had no knowledge of the desperate situation to our north. Now in full swing, the Battle of the Bulge called our names. It was time to answer.

Chapter 14

So Low, Looking Up At Down!

The Battle of the Bulge

One Goes, Another Returns

Severe blood clots in the legs removed our commanding officer, Captain Don Benedict, from the field for good.[1] His war was over. Lieutenant Mateyko again stepped into the vacancy, this time on a permanent basis.[2]

My old platoon leader, Lieutenant Bruno Rakowski returned to our outfit after a lengthy hospital stay. We were all happy to see him. The man could fight! He took over his old platoon and got right back to business.[3]

Coffee Anyone?

The 94th Division relieved us, so we continued to retrace our steps west.[4] We again crossed the Moselle River. Officers then oddly ordered us to remove all means of identification, excluding dog tags. We painted over insignias and vehicle numbers, removed shoulder patches and burned all personal letters. Top brass wanted no one, especially the enemy, to know that the entire 90th Division was on the move north, to the Ardennes.

The winter of 1944/1945 was brutal. Frigid throughout, temperatures often dropped below zero. A bitter wind howled and sang a steely song, cut and tore at all exposed flesh. It seemed to snow every day and not a little, but a lot. Total accumulation bogged things down as inches added into feet. And by early January, it had only begun.

Our caravan pushed steadily toward the Bulge. Near Luxembourg City, we found ourselves in the midst of a traffic jam. Although trucks hauled most, I rode shotgun in an open jeep with an attached half-ton trailer.

Cold beyond belief, we tried to make the best of it—tried not to dwell on it. The pause afforded us ample time to whip up some really bad coffee. From the Germans, we'd taken an enormous propane tank, connected to a blowtorch. It served as our energy source. We soon heated a can full of snow into a rolling boil. In true Army fashion, Supply always issued five-gallon containers of coffee with no way to brew it. Without a filter, I just threw a couple of dirty handfuls of the grounds into the mix. Be assured, frontline coffee was not the gourmet variety; it lacked any hint of refinement.

The propane tank sprang a leak and began to whistle and holler. Afraid she might blow, guys panicked! No man wanted his war obituary to read, "died while making coffee." When the two soldiers holding the tank raced for cover, it fell over atop our trailer. Blankets and packs quickly caught fire.

We frantically chucked all burning items, tank included, over a nearby stone wall. The smoldering debris slid down a hill and clanked to rest at the bottom. Thankfully, the snow not only doused the flames, but also, smothered the impending explosion.

What a circus! But, it served as a welcome diversion

from the cold. Although it wasn't quite the atmosphere of a romantic European cafe, we did enjoy some lukewarm, last-rate coffee—in a traffic jam—in an open jeep—in the middle of a driving snowstorm—on our way to the Battle of the Bulge.

"Get Out!"

Shortly after Luxembourg City, most men, with the exception of our unlucky jeep drivers, loaded into 2.5-ton trucks. The snow-choked roads severely slowed travel. Well south of Bras, we began to hear the familiar sounds of artillery fire. As the "booms" ramped up in volume, the truckers had heard enough. They pulled into a line along the roadside and stopped.

Dropped far from our objective, we weren't happy! While some haggled with the drivers to keep them occupied, others cleaned out each truck's digging arsenal. We grabbed picks, axes and shovels from their undersides. Our needs justified our means—at least, that's how we placated our consciences. After all, we were the ones who had to bust into the frozen tundra.

The sounds of their motors faded into the distance and our surroundings fell eerily silent. We saw no houses, barns or shelters of any kind. Covered in a thick blanket of pure white snow, the hills and trees looked down on us ominously. Perhaps a deadly winter now ranked as our greatest foe.

Immediately, we moved out in an effort to gain ground in dark's early hours. The march forward, through deep snow with full field packs, proved terribly tough. We made minimal progress before falling out to dig in—an impossible order to follow. We scratched and clawed throughout the night with little success. A dirty, gray sky marked morning as we again pushed north, toward the enemy.

Carnage lined the roadways along the Belgium-Luxembourg border. Pictured here, newly fallen snow covers an American ambulance destroyed by German fire – January 1945.

A Night's Worth Of Recon

South of Bras, I was ordered to recon ahead. Our maps of this region were a mess, so we needed some eyes-on intelligence. I set out with a small squad in search of anything I could find—natural landmarks, known roads, enemy numbers and locations.

Reconnaissance work was never more difficult than at the Bulge. For one, against the white backdrop, our uniforms stuck out like print on a newspaper. German units along the way would have little trouble spotting us. Moreover, the knee-deep drifts not only slowed foot travel, but also rendered many roads and landmarks unidentifiable. Evening's approach only added to our worries.

Before we departed, our artillery observer requested a moment of our time. Firsthand, he delivered a sales pitch regarding an experimental shell, fresh on the market.

180

Each new round was wired with a proximity switch to detonate it some six to eight feet above the surface, instead of on impact. A combination artillery shell and a cluster bomb, it was a nice idea, but sounded too good to be true, especially for the Army.

We received sniper fire almost immediately. It first came from our left, along a tree line. I radioed in for some of that new and improved artillery support. The rounds screamed through the air, but instead of popping at head height, they exploded high above, fifty to eighty feet from the target. It made for one hell of a fireworks show, but did little against enemy emplacements.

We struggled on, while sporadic fire spun us around, chased us from this side to that. Momentarily clear, we took refuge in a burnt-out farmhouse. Only the walls remained. Apart from the nag of enemy bullets, I paused to compare my map and compass with what I saw.

Hungry as hell, I also hurriedly downed a K-ration, my one and only for the day. We'd been fighting a losing battle with dysentery for months. Accordingly, my bowels rioted against this latest intrusion and sent me streaking from the structure. Out back within a copse of trees, I found an adequate place to conduct my business. While there, I noticed several large lumps in the snow. I scooped and scraped to uncover a handful of dead GIs.

Clearly they were not killed in action, but afterward, execution style. The enemy apparently took issue with their carrying German side arms as souvenirs. Although top brass warned us of the dangers, we all did it. The captors had stuck a pistol in each prisoner's mouth and fired, then left the weapon and horrible expression behind, both frozen in place and time on each murdered man's face.

Worried that the gang capable of these horrible crimes might still be in the neighborhood, I advised my team to ditch any and all German paraphernalia. I myself stood guilty as charged, in possession of two Walthers P38s at the time. I hated to bury such beautifully crafted weapons under a pile of trash, but my life meant more to me than contraband pistols.

Snipers again picked up our scent and forced us along. I've often wondered how much of the fire we caught that night was friendly. Small pockets of Americans and Germans lay intermingled throughout the countryside, often unaware of each other, friend or foe.

We finally arrived on a sizable blacktop. The road ran south of Bras to connect Bastogne with Wiltz. We crossed over, then tiptoed along the village's east side, careful not to cause a commotion. Armed with a mental picture, I radioed our findings back to Battalion. Two things stood out. The surrounding forests were incredibly thick and Bras was full of Krauts. We saw several manned emplacements.

The sun soon peaked over the eastern horizon. Our unit joined us, ready for a fight. They wouldn't be disappointed.

Absent Mind Over Matter

We initially engaged the enemy in the wildly tangled woods, southeast of Bras, along the Belgium-Luxembourg border. Amid the trees, buried in knee-deep snow, Jerry patiently awaited our arrival. Hidden under white camouflage coverings, they coaxed us in, then cut us down. The pale capes worked marvelously. If the Germans hadn't opened fire, we may have walked right through them. Caught by surprise, we suffered several casualties before we could even react. Whether wounded or not, all sought refuge in the snow.

But instead of floundering about, we forged ahead. It was a game of pressure. We watched their gun blasts, returned fire and advanced forward. Soon it was they who were on the defensive. White snow, now stained blood red, blanketed the small battlefield. Our part in the Battle of the Bulge had begun.

Citizens work to clear debris from the battle-weary border town of Trois Viergas, Luxembourg – January 1945.

Well-stocked, our enemy not only brought infantry to spare, but also artillery, mortars and tanks. The exchanges surrounding Bras were exceedingly violent. We traded blows, back and forth, not for minutes, but for days. I fired for hours at a time, with few pauses between.

In a move from one fighting position to the next, I noticed the familiar smell of burnt flesh. Believe me, once you come to know its odor, you'll never forget it. Moments later, I felt the pain in my hand. In the heat of battle, I'd mistakenly grabbed my gun's searing hot barrel instead of the stock. My palm and fingers were blistered badly, but I just buried my hand in the snow for a bit, then got back to business.

I've always marveled at how my nose alerted me to the problem before my hand. Maybe the mental and physical drain dulled some of the senses—absent mind over matter.

Goodbye Old Friend

After a very full day, we set up for the night. A fortunate few of us happened on a large, abandoned dugout. Branches and limbs topped with dirt provided overhead shelter from the falling snow and relentless wind. It was frigid, dark and cramped, but the best thing going. An easy dozen took refuge within.

Foxholes littered the small field in front. Each contained a ready supply of dead Germans. For safety's sake, we checked them all—a truly morbid task. Overhead artillery had apparently saturated the area and rained down on an unsuspecting enemy. I'd never seen so many head wounds in all my days. Some Allied spotter really earned his pay for that cache. Dozens of lifeless bodies, death frozen on their faces, filled the holes to capacity.

Huddled in the dugout, we leaned on each other for warmth and security. Quarters were close, but no one complained. At least, we had some semblance of a roof over our heads.

My old friend, Sergeant Herbert Roeglin sat directly in front of me. We'd been buddies since our days in the

States. He hailed from the farm country of St. James, Minnesota. Two Midwestern boys in a sea of Southerners, we had hit it off right from the start. An outstanding soldier and tremendously nice guy, he often spoke of life "back home."

Sergeant Herbert Roeglin, at home on the farm near St. James, Minnesota, prior to war.

We all sat on our butts, fairly upright, packed like sardines. My back pressed firmly against the rear dirt wall. Roeglin sat between my legs, his back against my chest.

The enemy soon began throwing round after round of artillery into our locale. There was little we could do, except wait it out. We shuddered in cold darkness as the earth quaked and trees burst all around us.

Roeglin and I caught up on old times, but then, it happened. A shell landed too close. It shook our bunker to its foundation. Much of the dirt and part of the roof fell in, but everyone appeared all right.

Yet, when I spoke to Roeglin, he failed to answer. A piece of shrapnel had struck the good sergeant and killed him instantly. Amid the jumbled noise and confusion, I hadn't even noticed. I don't remember a shriek, a gasp or even a word. He was just gone.

I sat in silence, quiet disbelief. I held him close, clutched my comrade for what seemed like forever, but no amount of desire could bring back the dead.

I laid my fallen friend there in the snow, flanked by woods and fields, somewhere east of Bras. Out of respect, I covered him with a blanket. Or maybe, I didn't want him to get cold. I knelt down, patted him on the chest, sobbed "Goodbye old friend," and walked back into battle.

I've since returned twice to visit his grave at the American Military Cemetery at Luxembourg City. He had so much to offer this world. Why was I spared and he taken? To my last breath, I'll never forget Sergeant Herbert Roeglin.

M Company Photo by David Pond Willis

Sergeant Herbert Roeglin
M Company, 358th Infantry
KIA – January 13, 1945 Battle of the Bulge

A Trio Of Purple Hearts

He was far from alone. Amid heavy casualties, we pushed north, along the eastern side of the village. We spent several days slugging it out, on and around a group of railroad tracks. The encounters were chaotic and continuously intense.

On January 15, Sergeant Allan McInnis and his machine-gun crew were in the midst of buttoning up another bunker, when he again felt the sting of enemy steel. This time, McInnis took a Kraut bullet in the worst of locations. The round cut through the right side of his neck, severed his trachea, scraped the top of his left lung, then exited just below his armpit.

Buddies pause for a picture shortly before the
Battle of the Bulge – December 1944.
Left to right: unknown, Hobert Winebrenner, Allan McInnis

"I'd been hit before, so I knew what it was," McInnis later described. "But when I started coughing up blood, I knew it was bad. I passed out. I came to as they were taking me out on a stretcher. A North Carolinian named George Harrell came up to say good-bye and wish me luck. I'll never forget it. I passed out again and when I regained consciousness, I was in a field hospital. They had put a tracheotomy tube in so I could breathe. There was a nurse sitting beside my bed. She worked a hand-operated suction device that kept the mucus from building up in my breathing tube. I went from Paris, directly to the States. It was at least five months before I could even talk, which was hard because I was a horrible speller." [5]

Three times proved the charm for McInnis. After nearly a year in and out of various hospitals, he returned home with his trio of Purple Hearts. Saco, Maine's gain was our loss. Few were better in battle than McInnis, but his war was over.

Day By Day

We'd been at it for several days in and around Bras, battling subzero temperatures as well as Germans. Deep snow turned the most mundane tasks into monumental undertakings. Beyond battle casualties, trench foot and frostbite crippled our ranks, shrank our numbers. Mentally and physically spent, we fought well under-strength.

At night, we attempted to dig in, but a really worthy foxhole was almost impossible to excavate. When temperatures dropped so low that shovels no longer worked, we resorted to explosives. C-4 broke the ground into large chunks, which we then tossed from the craters.

Although holes quickly filled with snow and ice, you were at least below the wind and flying metal. That hole in the ground might just be enough to see you through the night, that is, if you didn't freeze to death. Once down in, you never wanted to leave its security, but the battle always beckoned.

The long, cold nights were also tough on our equipment. Laid in the snow, communication lines became brittle and cracked. Several times, we discovered it the hard way. Some frantic calls for support never made it through.

U. S. Army Signal Corps Photo, Courtesy National Archives

Two members of the 90th Infantry Division check for damaged telephone lines through the snow-covered border town of Benonchamps, Belgium – January 1945.

Frigid temperatures froze and locked weapons. Rifles were the worst. Mechanisms such as bolt action often refused to budge. At times, you had to literally kick the lug to break it loose. Some guys resorted to urinating on their weapons. The warmth temporarily thawed things out. The Bulge was all about survival and you did whatever it took.

Run For Red Delicious

We finally scored a couple of days off-line and moved back for some warmth and rest. Sergeant Howard Pemberton received a well-deserved battlefield commission, but little actually changed. He had been leading his platoon for months. The promotion to lieutenant only made his leadership role official. Two silver stars and a battlefield commission, all within a seven-week period—not too bad for a Missouri farm boy.

M Company Photo by David Pond Willis

Howard Pemberton
M Company, 358th Infantry

"Come and get it!" the kitchen crews called for hot chow. The very idea put a little bounce in our step as we approached the trucks. A worker handed me a loaded mess kit, packed tight with chicken, mashed potatoes, peas, jello and pudding. I found a seat in the snow to enjoy the meal. I jumped into the chicken like a hyena on a carcass, only to find feathers on it. Gross! It was too disgusting, even for me! And that's saying something, because I was starving! I tossed that plateful and settled for a serving of mashed potatoes.

Around the kitchen, I also caught wind of an apple shipment to the south and readily volunteered my services. At the Bulge, something as simple as a piece of fresh fruit could make a GI's day, or maybe even a week. Another soldier and I borrowed a jeep and slipped out on a run for Red Delicious. We met up with the apples as planned, but they were all frozen and had been for sometime—no good to anyone. We were crushed.

Our morale completely bottomed out when on the way home, we passed several burial crews. Men and machines scooped out long trenches and filled them first with dead, then dirt. I can still see lines of 2.5-ton trucks, packed to the sideboards with frozen corpses.

Even off-line, supplies ran late, short or not at all. Near Bras, we were scheduled to receive gasoline and batches of new, wool, winter socks. They were coming by air from England. For men in our situation, it was a huge deal. Nobody cared about the fuel, but the socks may as well have been bars of gold. Finally, something warm for our feet!

Sure enough, a couple of cargo planes soon buzzed into our air space. They first dropped the gasoline, five-gallon cans stacked on pallets. But they weighed way too much for the size of their chutes and crashed to the ground. The containers burst to throw fuel everywhere. It was a total loss, but as I said before, no one cared. We had socks on our minds.

The planes circled and came in lower still. From the cargo doors, crews pushed several large bundles. The bunches bounced, hopped and tumbled along the ground before coming to rest. At least twenty of us pursued longingly as if we were aiming at the arms of wives or girlfriends. We ripped open the packages, only to find despair. Shoulders drooped and jaws dropped in disbelief. Instead of heavy wool winter socks, Supply mistakenly sent us the light summer variety—little dainty white ankle-cut things that women wear while playing tennis.

Cooler heads saw the value in them anyway, but they didn't prevail. Tempers ran hot! Actions turned violent! Distraught GIs first poured machine-gun fire into the unsuspecting bundles, then backed off a bit to toss in grenades. We really taught those summer socks a lesson. Although pointless, the juvenile display did take our minds off freezing for a few minutes.

Bastogne Bound

Back at it again, we continued along the Belgium-Luxembourg border to the town of Niederwampach. The tide of the Bulge had turned. German strategy shifted from conquer to escape. With weapons ready and eyes wide-open, we whacked anything Kraut trying to filter back through to the motherland.

U. S. Army Signal Corps Photo, Courtesy National Archives

Two 358th Infantry, 81mm mortar observers work their craft near Oberwampach, Luxembourg – January 1945.

After several more days in the cold and snowy wilderness, we received orders for Bastogne. I scouted ahead with a motorized recon team to make sure the path remained clear. This time, there was no sniper fire or frenzied dash from tree to tree, but instead, a journey through all that the Bulge was—miles of death and destruction.

U. S. Army Signal Corps Photo, Courtesy National Archives

Bound for Bastogne, a 90th Division ambulance passes by a knocked-out enemy tank – January 1945.

The entire region lay in shambles with wrecked, smoldering vehicles of all makes and models as common as natural landscaping. You wouldn't believe all the junked tanks and burnt-out trucks. Frozen, mangled corpses, Axis and Allied alike, poked from the snow.

We stumbled on an abandoned American aid station. Most likely, our enemy overran it in the early stages of battle. Dozens of once wounded GIs now lay stiff and silent in death, still on their stretchers.

Later along the way, we noticed a line of horse-drawn wagons, partially hidden behind an outcropping of trees. Well-made with canvas tops and rubber tires, most carried an extra team of horses, no doubt looted along the way.

Few in number, we approached cautiously. The horses appeared content, but the Kraut drivers had seen better days. One after another, dead, dead, dead—they were all dead. Some still sat in position, while others had fallen to the ground. It must have been one hell of an ambush. Their cargo included captured K-rations and American medical supplies. But thankfully, they never got the chance to use them.

Anywhere else, I would have been shocked, but not at the Bulge. This kind of stuff was everywhere! Fire and ice—the entire region had an apocalyptic feel to it.

U. S. Army Signal Corps Photo, Courtesy National Archives

Burnt-out enemy armor marked the
route to Bastogne – January 1945.

Bastogne was beaten down badly, but still standing. The battle had left her streets long ago. She now served as a forward hub for the entire region.

While there, we received a startling amount of replacements. Don't get me wrong, we were ecstatic to have the extra help! It's just that their numbers so dwarfed ours, we were happy, and a little worried, all at the same time. With the veteran to new guy ratio overwhelmingly skewed in their favor, we didn't know quite how to handle them all. They'd have to learn on the fly.

Bastogne was bustling! American soldiers, from all different units, were everywhere you turned. Medics, Supply guys, MPs, kitchen crews, GIs fresh from the front—they were all there. We billeted in a schoolhouse, which compared to where we'd been staying, felt like a five-star hotel.

U. S. Army Signal Corps Photo, Courtesy National Archives

A view from above looking down into the hustle and bustle of Bastogne – January 1945.

A Winter To Remember

By all accounts, the Battle of the Bulge was over. It had moved full circle from American debacle to hard-earned victory, but at an enormous cost. In less than a month, our Battalion alone suffered 296 casualties.[6] A huge number, considering that fresh from Koenigsmacker, Butzdorf and Dillingen, we entered the fray at far from full strength.

When a battalion's size is measured in dozens of men, rather than hundreds, something has gone terribly wrong, and that was the Bulge. There just wasn't anyone left. Prior to our mass restocking at Bastogne, only a skeleton crew remained.

Although the fighting proved fierce, it's to the weather that my mind most often returns. You can't imagine the suffering. As for proper clothing, we just didn't have it, or not nearly enough of it. The Army dropped the ball and GIs paid the price. While online, I remember shivering uncontrollably, hour after hour, day by day.

Our boots didn't get the job done either. Maybe we asked too much of them. Continually buried in snow, our feet were always wet. I'd never seen so many black toes in all my life. Frostbite and trench foot sent more GIs from the field than enemy bullets.

There were instances when we actually cut up portions of our blankets and tied them with twine around our feet. We wrapped paper, cardboard, whatever we could get our hands on, around our upper torsos as insulation. We came to know firsthand what Washington's men must have felt like at Valley Forge. Some aspects of soldiering had changed little, even in 170 years.

Dysentery ran rampant. In varying degrees, every man suffered from a cold or pneumonia. We weren't eating. We weren't sleeping. Our bodies and minds were shutting down. But still, we carried on. I witnessed GIs stay online, when they belonged in a hospital. I saw men refuse to take their boots off because they knew they'd never get them back on again.

The Bulge wasn't about the American Flag or even God above. It was about that guy beside you—that sorry shivering soldier, and those in the next foxhole, and so on, and so forth, down the line. For me, they stuck it out. For them, I refused to quit. Bonds formed at the Bulge will never be broken.

Goodbye Bulge, Hello Germany

In late January 1945, we left Bastogne to roll back into Luxembourg. The snow followed, heavy as usual. Multiple days of sporadic firefights led us to the banks of the Our River. As we crossed over into Germany, we opened a new door. But more importantly, we closed an old one behind us.

U. S. Army Signal Corps Photo, Courtesy National Archives

Along with 6th Armored Division half-tracks, 90th Division troopers tromp through the Luxembourg countryside – January 1945.

Even during the winters of today, I look out from the comfort of my home, across fields covered in snow and I'm there again—back at the Bulge. I can still see the fox-holes filled with soldiers, helmet nubs inching above the surface. Sixty years have passed, but it feels like yester-day.

Old soldier returns to the scene. Hobert Winebrenner visits the Battle of the Bulge Memorial outside Bastogne – 1970.

It was one of the worst times of my life. Several of us kept repeating an old saying that fit perfectly, "Lord, I'm so low, I declare, I'm looking up at down!" Yet, we had sur-vived. Goodbye Bulge! Hello Germany!

Chapter 15

Run To The River

Our River to Rhine River, Germany

Crashing A Dinner Party

February brought a welcome warm spell and heavy rains. Feet of snow melted into a giant mud bog. Roads turned to soup.

We pushed east, village by village. Some surrendered with little resistance, while others fought to the bitter end.

Occasionally, we caught the enemy completely by surprise. Just in country, we entered one house to find a hot meal still on the table. The Kraut officers had fled in such a rush that they left their coats on the chair backs. We threw the jackets onto the table and grabbed the cloth at the corners. Like bulls in a china shop, we heaved the entire mess through the kitchen window. We then reset the table, raided the basement for food, tossed some furniture into the fire and enjoyed a nice little dinner.

When unable to scrounge food to our liking, we sometimes settled for a concoction dubbed "GI gruel." Simply sweet and somewhat filling, it amounted to cracked wheat and condensed milk, boiled in with candy. Although nothing near Mom's cooking, it served its purpose. You took what you could get.

U. S. Army Signal Corps Photo, Courtesy National Archives

90th Division vehicles slide through the flooded Our River Valley – February 1945.

My Lice Raft

Throughout winter and the Bulge, when not wearing my helmet, I donned a rabbit-skin cap, liberated from a German POW. For many, it became an endless source of amusement and really took on a life of its own.

As the weather warmed, one joker prodded, "Are you going to wear that lice-ridden thing the whole year?"

"Guess not!" I replied and threw it into the river. Fairly rank by then, the hat had lived a rich, full life atop my head. But, it was time for it to move on.

Spectators watched and laughed as it skimmed along the top of the water. Then guys opened fire, yelling, "It's a monster! Kill it before it grows and eats Chicago!"

Sergeant Hobert Winebrenner with muddy boots and rabbit-skin cap – February 1945.

One soldier even set up his light machine gun and poured half a belt through. Pot shots riddled my poor lice raft. After much of the 3rd Battalion had taken a turn, our regimental CO, Colonel Bealke, drove up in his jeep. He was good with faces and remembered mine from our earlier days in France.

"No trouble," we assured him. "Just guys letting off a little steam."

Bealke sent a glance my way, but I couldn't tell if it was a smirk or a frown. By that time, the higher-ups treated us sergeants pretty well. Deadly attrition had so decimated our officer pool that NCOs played a major role in running the show.

Bouncing Betty's

Ever forward, in the second week of February, we stumbled into the most delicate of situations. Before we realized it, dozens of us had wandered well into an enemy minefield. The initial explosions not only marked our latest casualties, but also tipped us off to our predicament.

Many of the mines were "Bouncing Bettys," nasty little contraptions. Often homemade, they were simple, but deadly. They amounted to loosely buried steel cans, filled with a combination of explosives and metal fragments. A propellant, when triggered, popped the container into the air, where it detonated to throw its jagged contents, often nails, with amazing force. If the shrapnel didn't kill you, it surely messed you up.

We quickly changed gears from overdrive to neutral. If you weren't hit, you stayed put. The sweepers combed the area, then helped us through. They hastily marked the mines, while we traced the bootprints of the guys ahead of us. If you looked closely, you could tell where the devices lay, see the freshly worked soil. Scary! Scary! Scary!

Back At The Siegfried Line

From the minefield, we jumped back into the jaws of the Siegfried Line—pillboxes and dragon's teeth as far as the eye could see. It reminded me of November 1944— our worst nightmare revisited.

U. S. Army Signal Corps Photo, Courtesy National Archives

358th Infantry soldiers surge through the dragon's teeth of the Siegfried Line – February 1945.

We fought a tremendously violent, three-day rolling battle from Winterscheid to Brandscheid to Watzerath. Although there were plenty of enemy infantry, artillery and tanks, the enormous number of pillboxes gave us the most trouble. We took them one at a time—buttoned them up, then blew them out. But all the while, we suffered significant casualties in return.

Apart from Company M dead, Talmadge Floyd and Arthur Mathabel, the loss of two key leaders proved a terrible blow.[1] Shrapnel from an enemy round hit Lieutenant

Howard Pemberton so severely in the feet and lower legs that it ended his war. If you couldn't walk, you couldn't fight. Less than a month into his commission, he was homeward bound.[2]

U. S. Army Signal Corps Photo, Courtesy National Archives

A 358th Infantry soldier stands outside a secured Siegfried Line pillbox – February 1945.

Among many others, Company L's commanding officer was also wounded and removed from the field. Deservedly high on the Battalion depth chart, Lieutenant Rakowski was plucked from our ranks to fill the vacancy. Although selfishly sorry to see him go, I knew "L" would be better for it.

U. S. Army Signal Corps Photo, Courtesy National Archives
Two 3rd Battalion riflemen walk through the ruins of Brandscheid, while a covered corpse lays in the foreground – February 1945.

Tragically, Lieutenant Rakowski never realized his full potential. Just days after he assumed leadership, enemy rounds scored a direct hit on Company L's command post.[3] Information was always limited. Through the grapevine, we heard that Rakowski was severely wounded, took shrapnel from head to toe, but was still alive. That's all we knew. I never saw him again, and over the years, have often wondered whatever became of this man who fought so bravely.

On the ruble-strewn streets of Brandscheid, soldiers of the 3rd Battalion, 358th Infantry stare into a bomb crater at a dead enemy trooper – February 1945.

In a matter of days, we had lost two outstanding line leaders, Pemberton and Rakowski. Sure, they'd be replaced, but their shoes could never be filled. Sergeants stepped up and replacement officers learned on the go. As always, life and the war moved on.

U. S. Army Signal Corps Photo, Courtesy National Archives

The 90th Division rolls through what's left of Lunebach, Germany, near Watzerath – February 1945.

In retrospect, Company M was truly blessed with some great officers. Captain Marsh was one of the finest and obviously taught his subordinates well. Four of our young lieutenants, Benedict, McHolland, Mateyko and Rakowski, battle-hardened in the hedgerows of Normandy, all went on to command their own companies. We underlings were fortunate indeed.

In the middle of February, we moved back to Habscheid, Germany, for a few well-deserved days off. We ate hot meals, watched movies and nursed ailments. We were dry for the first time in weeks. Apart from the mud and enemy artillery fire, I really liked Habscheid.

U. S. Army Signal Corps Photo, Courtesy National Archives

A 90th Division jeep slops through
Habscheid, Germany – February 1945.

Bazooka Hobert?

Fresh from our vacation, we jumped back into battle. Masthorn, Arzfeld, Windhausen, Krautscheid, Bellscheid and Waxweiler all quickly fell by the wayside as we rumbled through Germany at an accelerated pace. In fact, we secured eleven towns in a 72-hour period.[4]

Oftentimes, I reconnoitered a village or two ahead for a preview of events to come. On one such occasion, in addition to my regular team, I grabbed a bazooka crew. We'd already encountered German armor in the area and they tended to be a little aggressive. I didn't want to take any chances.

The village felt strange from the start. Eerily silent, she

appeared completely deserted, not only void of German soldiers, but also civilians. The homes were nice, very well built. About four blocks in, we stopped abruptly. My old Indian friend, Simon Arthur thought he heard something. With my clenched fist raised in the air, we all crouched quietly and listened to icy rain peck at our helmets. And then, there it was—the faint but consistent drone of enemy armor. We scrambled into one of the houses and waited. Sure enough, the tank turned the corner and headed down our street, the main avenue.

M Company Recon Team, ready to roll.
Front row left to right: Winebrenner, Bennett, Arthur

As recon, we could have just trickled from town without a fight. But how much fun would that be? The tank driver was alone, at least for the moment. When circumstances offered you enemy armor on a platter, you graciously accepted.

I was always up for trying new things. Still a kid at heart, I was just wired that way. Full of eager anticipation,

I asked our bazooka man, "How about giving me a go at firing that thing?" With only the one enemy piece in town, what could it hurt?

A narrow hallway stretched straight from the front to the back door. We opened both, in an effort to free the weapon's rear blast.

The tank approached and I knelt on one knee with the bazooka to my shoulder. In hope of disabling the vehicle with a direct hit, I aimed at what I knew to be a vulnerable point—a sprocket near the rear idler wheels. I'd seen it done many times before and was anxious to gain some firsthand experience.

The unsuspecting tank pulled even. I squeezed the trigger and swoosh went the shell. Almost immediately, it veered left, missed the whole damn thing and blew the corner off the house across the street.

"Let's get out of here!" rang the choir.

Before the dust even settled, we darted out that rear door and sprinted through backyard gardens to take up residence in a home some ten houses down from our original position. That's when the flak really started flying. No, not from the German tank, but from my own men! They thought it hilarious that I had missed that thing at point-blank range and were determined not to let me live it down. They couldn't wait to get home to "M" and tell the guys about "Bazooka Hobert." We all enjoyed a good laugh.

Defective Ammo, Anyone?

To this day, I contend that it was a defective shell, loaded too heavy on one side. I'd seen it happen before, to folks a lot more experienced than I. We also had problems with bad mortar rounds. Some blew as soon as they hit the bottom of the tube. The wayward blasts took out entire crews. Whenever able, they sandbagged, but typically, there wasn't time.

Shortly after the war, a congressional team investigating flawed ammunition contacted me. They wanted eyewitnesses to testify in Washington. Although I didn't attend because of an operation involving my son, I believe 1st Sergeant Inman may have. I probably wouldn't have gone anyway. I'm sure it was a bureaucratic dog-and-pony show, a bunch of meetings culminating in nothing more than a cover-up. Anyway, a defective round was the story I was selling, but nobody was buying. Rightfully, we all continued to have some fun at my expense.

Tanker Panics

After I calmed down the comedy team, we watched for the tanker's next move. As expected, he reversed course and settled in front of our former address. Ready! Aim! Fire! With his machine gun on rapid and his 88 blowing holes clean through, he destroyed the structure. I'm glad we weren't home. Once he felt comfortable that life no longer existed on the first two floors, he swung his cannon to the rear and rammed what was left of the house. It was a common means to crush basement survivors.

We'd seen enough. Our bazooka crew aimed and this time it was they who fired. The shell hit dead on and pushed the tanker into a panic. He gunned the motor and threw his left track off. Then he held it wide-open and spun in circles, while firing full speed ahead. I've never heard an engine pitch that high. It wasn't long before the motor blew. His day was done.

In seconds, the turret hatch opened. Along with several puffs of smoke emerged a white flag, held with raised hands. Before we could even react, we again heard the familiar hum of approaching enemy tanks. It was time to go! In saying goodbye, we fired a few passing shots, just to shake them up. By the time we reached the crest of the hill beyond town, we started to receive machine-gun fire from the newly arrived armor. The bullets slapped harmlessly into the mud as we scrambled over the top and down the other side, happily on our way home, free and alive.

Schlafen Nicht Gut

A few days down the road, we again reconnoitered ahead into a small village. A river rambled directly through town to split it in two. The near side contained a fair amount of oddly shaped, old and dilapidated buildings that resembled peasant or tenant housing. Much newer and nicer homes graced the opposite bank. The river appeared to serve as, not only a geographic divide, but also as a social-economic barrier. Our unit planned on crossing over the next morning, so we were there for a quick walk-through.

Recon Regulars, Bennett and Winebrenner
pause for a picture – February 1945.

We began by nosing around the poorer side of town. A dim light peaked from a window of the second house. I gingerly spanned its creaking porch. As I reached for the handle, the door opened. In the threshold stood a frail old man, directly in front of me. He held a lantern, but raised it no higher than his waist. I peered past him to notice several enemy soldiers sleeping soundly on his floor.

"Schlafen zie?" he asked, motioning inside. In the dark, he mistook me for a German and offered me a place to spend the night.

"Schlafen nicht gut," I mumbled under my breath as I lunged for the latch and quietly closed the door.

We got out of there in a hurry and raced back to the hilltop. I immediately rang our mortar platoon and asked for a locating round. It hit down river. I brought him back and to the right. The new shell smacked the road directly in front of the tired home. Close enough! I called for effect and they dropped all six tubes onto that row of structures. We stuck around to clean up the leftovers, but I don't recall many. I didn't like killing the old man, but sometimes civilians got in the way, especially when hosting enemy slumber parties.

An Icy Crossing

Even without Kraut presence, spanning the river would be difficult. The bridge was long gone. To get their retreating tanks across, the Germans rolled dozens of huge logs into the water. I didn't see any armor, so it must have worked.

In fact, I'd guess that tanks crossed more easily than men. The weather couldn't make up its mind between winter snow and spring rain. Instead it just spit ice and coated the makeshift bridge with a thin layer. You couldn't get any kind of footing on the slick and uneven logs. Loaded down with guns, ammunition and assorted other goodies, our first few volunteers fell in. That was enough for the rest of us. We just sat on our asses and scooted across. We still got wet, but only from the waist down.

On the other side lay an enormous dugout, really just a shelter for cows. A sizable herd remained within. We waited inside for the rest of our unit to cross. For warmth, we buried our lower halves beneath straw and dried out manure. It worked for a time, but the fumes from the cows became nauseating. Back in that hole, the foul air couldn't escape. It just hovered, thick and stagnant. Too much to take, the bovine gases eventually forced us on down the line.

Bugs! Bugs! Everywhere Bugs!

No doubt due to the previous night's mortar show, the more prosperous side of town was also deserted, which suited us just fine. We scattered into different houses and built fires for warmth. The home we chose happened to be already occupied by three dead German soldiers. Based on their state of decomposition, they appeared only recently deceased. Another American recon outfit had most likely whacked them within the last few days. They didn't bother us, so we didn't bother them.

We also used breaks like this to debug ourselves. Our clothes and bodies alike housed countless parasites. Without the time or means to keep clean, we lay largely defenseless against these microscopic enemies. Army-issued bug powder not only didn't work all that well, but also caused an irritating rash. Through trial and error, we found baking our clothes to be an able remedy.

Many kitchens, this one included, had both a stovetop and a cooking compartment below. We first started some grub, then took off our clothes and placed them in the oven.

Throughout the winter, I wore whatever I could find. It usually consisted of a couple of T-shirts, a long-under-wear top, a sweatshirt, a wool GI shirt, one to four stolen sweaters, my field jacket and two or three pairs of pants. My wardrobe alone filled the small opening. It didn't seem odd at the time, but now I look back and laugh at the thought of us, wrapped in blankets, sitting around a table, baking clothes, cooking food, all deep within enemy territory.

Once our attire reached well-done, we shook it out. You could actually see some of the bigger bugs flop off. Although only temporary, the warmth and relief felt tremendous.

Inside this house, we also witnessed bugs vacating one of the dead bodies. He must have had something. With their host now cold, the tenants searched for better accommodations. They were very small in size. We only noticed them because their color contrasted with the soldier's coat.

I'm amazed at how uncivilized we had become. We ate dinner with dead human beings lying at our feet. And perhaps most disturbing, it didn't faze us in the least! We watched bugs traverse a corpse as if we had tuned into our favorite television show. Although I didn't realize it then, war had changed me, and not for the better.

"Step Right In Sergeant!"

Our enemy often hovered on a village's outskirts to hit us with their big guns as we moved in. They held nothing back in pummeling their own towns, time and time again. As we surged into one such burg, German artillery hammered us from the distance. We scrambled for cover.

I busted my tail to the nearest house and barreled for its entrance. The home was sturdy and the door, even more so. It was solid oak with a strong bolt and handle. Of course, it wouldn't budge. I manned a carbine that day and threw multiple rounds into the latch-lock area. But when I tried it again, nothing! I even launched several well-placed kicks to no avail. They certainly got their money's worth for that door.

In real time, this all occurred over seconds. Enemy artillery fire accelerated our every action. One of my buddies soon tossed himself onto the porch and rolled to a stop at my feet. In addition to his government-issued weaponry, he always carried a long-barreled, 12-gauge shotgun, mailed over from home. He took one look at my face, then blew a sizable hole through the door. With the entire latch-lock area now gone, the door gently swung open on its hinges.

"Step right in, Sergeant!" he chuckled as we both raced for the basement.

While jeeps prepare to roll, a M Company Recon Team sets out on another mission – March 1945.

Steel-rim Glasses

That gun intrigued me to no end. Not only was it from home, which automatically made it better, but it was also modified for more power. The barrel had been bored out to accommodate larger rounds.

We took care of our Ordnance guys and in return, they saw to our special ammunition needs. We continually showered them with captured pistols, mainly lugars and P38s. In exchange, they machined shells for our more unique firearms. For that particular shotgun, they manufactured brass rounds loaded with "00" steel balls to give them lots of ass. Whenever they ran a batch of those, they also made up a box of solid lead slugs. At times, I believed that weapon to be our deadliest. It packed one mighty punch.

The kid in me had to have a go with that gun. I had experience with a myriad of weaponry, including carbines, M1s, BARs, the gamut of machine guns from light to heavy, air to water-cooled—all caliber, mortars and even bazookas, but I'd never fired anything quite like that shotgun.

That night, we hunkered down in a wide-open space between villages. Along with another recon regular, Simon Arthur and I set out for a quick peak into the next town. With my buddy's permission, I borrowed the souped-up 12-gauge.

We sidled in under the cover of darkness; the town seemed pretty well buttoned up. Arthur stalked parallel to my position, while our getaway guy brought up the rear, some fifteen feet behind. I peered down the first side street to see nothing but several doors. For a closer look, I proceeded into the alley. My hands strangled the shotgun. I held it at hip level. About halfway down, a door jumped open and out popped a rifle, shouldered to a soldier, ready to roll. The German glared over his gun sight through steel-rim eyeglasses. I'll never forget his face or those spectacles. I've spent many nights revisiting both in my sleep. He had me and pulled the trigger. Click! The rifle didn't fire! No shell occupied the chamber.

At nearly the same moment, I got a similar reaction from my weapon. Nothing! I forgot to cock the damn thing! I rightfully deserved to be shot for even taking that gun on patrol. One of the cardinal rules of recon was to be a creature of habit. Unfamiliarity often spelled disaster.

With my big dumb body in front of the German, Simon Arthur couldn't get a shot off either. By the time I got her cocked and ready, Arthur had already passed me by and forced the Kraut to the floor. The enemy soldier quietly surrendered without incident.

We could have easily blown him away, no questions asked. But since my life-altering experience in Normandy, I followed the rules. That German sergeant, who had rescued me from his own men, was fresh in my mind. Hell, he's still there today.

I returned the favor and instructed the young man to follow me. At the alley's entrance, I had him break his rifle against the building and toss his two potato-masher grenades through the storefront window.

He was part of a rear guard, in town to fight a delaying action. We ordered him to the middle of the street to call out to the rest of his comrades for their surrender. You never know if something will work unless you try it. After fifteen minutes, here they came, no helmets or weapons, hands atop their heads. We moved through town the next morning as if we owned the place.

My Indian Friend

Prior to my service, I knew no Indians. There just weren't any in rural Indiana. Those I met in the Army, I liked. But, one stood out in particular. Before it was all over, we'd become more than friends—almost brothers.

Simon Arthur was a full-blooded Arapaho. He hailed from Arapahoe, Wyoming, within the Wind River Indian Reservation. Quietly courageous, he took "winning the war" seriously and always performed above and beyond the call to duty. Yet, he wasn't obsessed. He had a life outside of war. You could see it in his eyes, feel it from his words.

A mainstay on my recon team, Arthur followed me through thick and thin. I never left home without him. He was calm, yet decisive—sturdy as well as steady. His character fit perfectly with that type of work. Our relationship was as comfortable as a pair of worn blue jeans. Without so much as saying a word, we knew what each other was thinking. I had his back and he, mine. It was just understood. Throughout late 1944 and early 1945, I trusted him with my life, most every day. He never let me down.

Simon Arthur
M Company, 358th Infantry

Sizzle and Swish

Nearer to the Rhine, the resistance stiffened. At Bretzenheim, we worked in the face of torrential enemy artillery fire. Much of it wasn't the regular float-in type, but rather the low, straight barreled, sizzle and swish variety, with umpteen hundred feet of velocity behind it.

I was scared! I'm sure we all were. The shells sliced men in two. With each step, I strongly desired to dive into the ground and plant myself until summer. But Mateyko wouldn't allow it—wouldn't let us. He was smart enough to know that if we did, we'd all die! We had to apply pressure. It was our only way out.

Replacements looked to the old-timers for guidance. If
we flinched in any way, the new guys would be asses and
elbows out of there—Paris-bound before blinking an eye.
Mateyko knew this and kept the veterans stomping forward. Like sheep to the slaughter, the others followed.

Throw in enemy infantry, mortars and anti-tank guns
and it was one hell of an all-day battle. Sergeant Bill
Masters was another M Company original that had been
transferred to "K." He earned the Distinguished Service
Cross that day for what the Army dubbed "fearless determination and courageous devotion." He didn't think too
much of it, nor did we, because he did things like that all
the time. We just termed it, "typical Masters." The official
citation read in part:

" ... *On 21 March 1945, during an assault against
Bretzenheim, Germany, Sergeant Masters' platoon was
pinned down by intense enemy machine-gun fire.
Accompanied by an automatic rifleman, Sergeant
Masters started forward to silence the gun. The rifleman
was hit but the intrepid Sergeant continued on alone,
worming his way forward under a hail of fire. He hurled a
hand grenade into the enemy position and killed the gunner, killed the assistant gunner when he attempted to
take over the gun and the noncommissioned officer in
charge when he tried to rally his men. Leaderless and
demoralized by Sergeant Masters' bold assault the rest of
the enemy crew surrendered to him. Sergeant Masters'
heroic action permitted his platoon to advance and seize
the town. ...*" [5]

Toward dusk, the Germans backed off the big guns. It
took a while to move those things and they weren't ready
to turn them over just yet. We secured the city that
evening, but had suffered dozens of casualties in the
process.

Mummified

The next morning, we rolled into Mainz, where the going proved much easier. We approached from the west as the bulk of our enemy pulled back across the Rhine River. Our Air Corps had so significantly softened the field that beyond ruble, little remained of the city. I've never witnessed a place so completely destroyed.

U. S. Army Signal Corps Photo, Courtesy National Archives

358th Infantry troopers comb the crater-filled streets of Mainz, Germany – March 1945.

We first worked through a suburb that had been burned to the ground. Our boys up above must have hit them with firebombs. Much like with our WP, once you got enough of that stuff on your skin, it was game over.

We happened on a German anti-aircraft unit. Dozens of 88's lined a city street with barrels pointed to heaven.

With the Luftwaffe in shambles, that crew must have stood as Mainz's last line of defense against an air assault. They fared none too well.

The scene made me sick. Many German soldiers still sat in position, at their posts to the horrific end. Caught by the firebombs, most were burned beyond recognition and more resembled ancient mummies than the young men they were only minutes earlier. The intense heat vaporized their uniforms, scorched their skin to the consistency of dried leather and literally burned them alive. Although I hated the enemy, I found myself feeling sorry for that lot and their uneasy deaths.

U. S. Army Signal Corps Photo, Courtesy National Archives

Mainz was not for the faint of heart! 90th Division GIs look on at a scorched German soldier, fried to the seat of his burned-out half-track – March 1945.

Hitler Youth

Throughout Mainz, the older locals, realizing that only formalities remained, cooperated fully. But, the "Hitler

Youth" provided some of the stiffest resistance. Those aspiring young terrorists refused to quit. They dug in deep, ready for war.

There was nothing quite like losing three or four friends to a kid with a rifle on a rooftop. Then the rosy-cheeked, peach-fuzzed-faced freaks had the nerve to smile at us, laugh and ask for a cigarette. Let me just say that some of those cocky little assassins needed extensive dental work by the time they made it back to the POW cage. One shouldn't openly gloat in killing his captors' friends.

Sergeant Winebrenner receives mail call in Mainz, Germany. A letter from home always put a smile on our faces – March 1945.

Recon To The Rhine

Dozens of blocks into the city, we stopped toward evening. I received orders to recon to the river. I grabbed Arthur and a getaway guy and we descended into the moonscape that once was Mainz.

Well into our journey, we spied a handful of AWOL German soldiers. With no weapons and clothed only in dirty rags, they'd given up on the war. They existed as shells of humanity, mentally and physically stretched to the limit. We did them a huge favor by taking them as prisoners. They'd live much better in a POW camp, than in a pile of ruble.

A bombed-out second-story apartment comes to mind. A man, woman and their child sat at a dinner table, the youngest still in a high chair. They looked so peaceful, so right, except they were as dead as dust. The explosion not only took half their building, but also their lives.

With the town flattened, we could see the Rhine from a good distance away. That was close enough for my taste. Urban warfare was tough, especially three against an entire rear guard. Happy with what we'd found, we returned to camp with our prisoners.

M Company Team goes over map and objectives.
Left to right: unknown, Winebrenner, Peterson,
Mateyko, Anderson - March 1945.

Across The Rhine

We'd experienced much in our trek through Germany to the Rhine River. We'd fought in and passed through countless villages, crossed over several rivers. In less time than it took us to escape Normandy, we had tackled half the motherland.

And now, there we stood, at the banks of the mighty Rhine. Perhaps more symbolic than anything else, our crossing meant much to both sides. For us, it marked the halfway point in conquering Germany. We were about to enter the final phase, one huge step closer to home. For them, it signaled another nail in the coffin. All knew their days were numbered. On March 24, 1945, on a bridgehead near Selzen, we walked across the Rhine River.[6]

Sergeant Hobert Winebrenner and M Company radio operator, Garold Anderson approach the Rhine River bridgehead – March 1945.

Chapter 16

Humanity At Its Worst

Leeheim to Waldmunchen, Germany

Look Out Below!

After crossing the Rhine, we collected in the vicinity of Leeheim, west of Darmstadt.[1] I'd never witnessed so much anti-aircraft weaponry in one place. Clearly, Patton aimed to protect that bridgehead at all costs.

The Luftwaffe dispatched what little air power they still possessed, but it didn't amount to spitting in the wind. The ground seized violently as countless cannons hurled flak at the enemy fighters. A near constant stream of metal flowed upward. The noise was deafening! Some planes disintegrated in a ball of fire, while others climbed altitude to escape. In either case, their bombs fell far from the mark. The bridge held! Thousands of American troops and their supporting armor poured over the Rhine.

On the ground, we worried more about falling debris

than German bombs. With so much volume heading up, surely some was destined to return. And it did! Huge projectiles plummeted from the sky at the force of gravity. We just tried to stay out of the way. No umbrella was stopping those raindrops. We dug in deep that night and waited it out. The next day, we began our second leg through Germany.

Where's The Burgermeister?

We crossed the Main River without incident to take the town of Mittelbuchen. We continued in a northeasterly direction through the south side of Frankfurt. As in western Germany, some Krauts surrendered without resistance, while others fought to their deaths.

U. S. Army Signal Corps Photo, Courtesy National Archives

Soldiers of the 358th Infantry test communications during the drive toward Frankfurt – March 1945.

With much experience, we developed a routine. After expelling the enemy from a village, we demanded all remaining locals to fall in line with the program. We always first rounded up the mayor or burgermeister and explained to him the facts of life. Residents were to drape white sheets and pillowcases from their windows and doorframes to signal their status.

In addition, citizens were to surrender all firearms and place them in a central location on the main street. I remember huge stacks of weapons, some over twelve feet high. We then added gasoline to the guns and set them ablaze.

U. S. Army Signal Corps Photo, Courtesy National Archives

Laying down the law, a 90th Division team talks with the mayor of Obernhausen, Germany – April 1945.

The final condition was the most important—deadly serious for both sides. If, after ridding the burg of enemy soldiers, our men caught any fire, we'd burn the village to the ground, no questions asked. Except for one memorable occasion, the deterrent worked without flaw.

Women Poured Into The Streets

Northeast of Frankfurt, we rumbled into Hirzenhain, Germany and liberated a large slave labor camp full of female Polish prisoners.[2] Women poured into the streets. Although gaunt and malnourished, they seized the moment and openly celebrated. Witnessing newfound freedom firsthand was such a rush, almost indescribable. Mere words can't do it justice. It struck deep, to the depths of our souls.

We jumped to a market across the way and ran the owner into the basement. We cleaned out that store and passed all kinds of food into the streets. I carried rings of something like bologna around my neck, broke off chunks and tossed them into the crowd. Seeing faces that had not smiled for years, sore from laughter, brought tears to our eyes. Even the most battle-hardened GI couldn't help but be moved.

The store owner actually found the nerve to return and complain about the manner in which he and his shop were being treated. We sat that old Kraut down and read him the riot act! He had watched the Germans exploit and abuse these women for who knows how long. He'd probably even gained financially from the whole deal. In few words, we informed him that he was lucky to be alive. A kick in the ass sent him back to the basement.

We soon funneled the women to the rear of our lines for further assistance. Many required medical attention, and all would need help in finding their way home. We didn't stay long in Hirzenhain, just enough to set the record straight.

It Never Got Any Easier

In early April, we entered the city of Vacha, Germany. The resistance was stiff, especially for this late in the game. We fought block by block throughout, until we reached a railroad yard on the far end. Although the town lay largely secure, enemy mortar and sniper fire continued along the tracks.

Machine gunners from "M" accompanied rifle units from "K" and "I." I worked with a section attached to the platoon of my old friend, Sergeant Bill Masters. With few able to match his courage, he was a good one to have on your side in the middle of a scrap.

M Company Photo by David Pond Willis

Sergeant Bill Masters
K Company, 358th Infantry
KIA – April 14, 1945 Vacha, Germany

Tragically, less than two weeks after earning the Distinguished Service Cross at Bretzenheim, Masters was killed at Vacha. An enemy sniper cut him down. By the time I got to him, his nose and cheeks were blackened from being pulled on a loose cinder sidewalk, out of the line of fire. With water from my canteen, I dabbed the smudges from my dead friend's face. No matter how many times I had done it before, losing a buddy never got any easier.

U. S. Army Signal Corps Photo, Courtesy National Archives

Going my way? Whenever able, to quicken the pace, 90th Division foot soldiers hitched a ride on anything that would roll, in this case, friendly armor – April 1945.

Setting A Town Ablaze

Next we entered Unterbreizbach, Germany.[3] We secured the town and put the "routine" in motion. But this time, there was a problem. Well after the German Army had gone, local residents fired on our forces.

Unterbreizbach had stepped over the line! Guys got unglued in a hurry! Battalion brought up incendiary grenades and spare fuel. Panicked citizens poured from town. Per orders, troopers from "K" and "L" burned the village to the ground.[4] Although not an active participant, I witnessed the torching firsthand.

Even in retrospect, we had to do it. We had to set a precedent or we'd be sniped in every burg to Czechoslovakia. Although sorry that it had to happen, I'm convinced it was our only alternative. Ultimately, it saved lives down the road.

For the next fifty miles, frantic folks, waving white sheets and pale pillowcases, met us before we even neared their villages. They'd obviously heard about the encounter and wanted to make certain to avoid a sequel. Along this stretch, the resistance wasn't light, but rather, nonexistent.

A Star Is Born!

It was also in April that we received some unexpected, yet welcome news. A member of our team would take part in a promotional bond drive back in the States—sort of a hero's tour. Surely an honor, it was a huge deal! That close to the end, one soldier's war would be over early.

If I remember right, I think we actually voted for the designee. It was not a task taken lightly. I'm sure the Army's PR people envisioned a rugged mouthpiece with star-like attributes. But we only considered one qualification–who deserved it most.

In the end, 1st Sergeant Paul Inman scored the victory. He earned his ticket home by his own sweat and blood. We picked the right man.

He toured throughout the United States with the "Heroes of Bastogne." With events, appearances and speeches, his plate was full. In Southern California, he mingled with Hollywood's hottest celebrities.

Rubbing elbows with the stars, 1st Sergeant Paul Inman laughs with Gracie Allen and George Burns.

In San Francisco, Inman met the mayor. He also played a round of golf at the nearby, but exclusive Pebble Beach Golf Club.[5]

A far cry from Canyon, Texas, Inman saw how the other side lived. But I'm sure he remained the same old sarge we all knew and loved—rock solid, with few frills.

1st Sergeant Paul Inman in San Francisco on the "Heroes of Bastogne" Bond Drive. In the middle of the front row is the city's mayor, Roger Lapham. Sergeant Inman stands immediately to Mayor Lapham's right, with hands clasped in front.

Striking Gold At Merkers
Merkers, Germany was known for its salt mines. In

234

securing the city, we heard bits and pieces about buried treasure, but failed to investigate. On point at the time, we were in a hurry.

Of course, one of the mines turned out to be much more than met the eye, a truly monumental discovery. As Russian troops readied to enter Berlin's perimeter and Allied bombs continued to fall on the city's center, the Third Reich relocated its vast monetary reserves from its besieged capital to an unassuming salt mine at Merkers. Over previous months, they'd transferred valuables by the truckloads.

U. S. Army Signal Corps Photo, Courtesy National Archives

This nondescript Merkers's salt mine contained Nazi riches beyond belief – April 1945.

The "gold room" was straight out of the storybooks. Sacks of ingots and specie literally covered the floor. Countless bags of gold bullion were measured in the hundreds of tons, alone worth over $800 million in today's dollars.[6]

The "gold room" contained bags of bullion, ingots and specie, stacked as far as the eye could see – April 1945.

Beyond gold, the stash held platinum, silver, plus currency of all kinds—5,000,000,000 German marks, 2,000,000 American dollars, 4,000,000 Norwegian pounds and 100,000,000 French francs to name a few.[7]

John A. Busterud, in his book, *Below The Salt*, detailed some of the more unique treasures. He wrote:

"Included in the collection were paintings by Rembrandt, Raphael, Van Dyck, Monet, Manet and Renoir. In addition to the many paintings there were Arras tapestries, a Titian Venus, original Goethe manuscripts and rare oriental carpets. The final inventory included thousands of items, ranging from single paintings to 2,300 folios of rare Durer prints and etchings." [8]

U. S. Army Signal Corps Photo, Courtesy National Archives

"Wintergarden," painted by French impressionist, Eduoard Manet, numbered among the vault valuables – April 1945.

Perhaps most disturbing were the countless containers full of personal property seized from individuals. The looted items ranged from dinnerware to jewelry to dental work.[9]

In today's dollars, rather than millions, the total take would easily be worth billions. Before long, Patton, Bradley and Eisenhower were all down in there, fingering through the booty. We chuckled at how it took a sensational photo opportunity to get three generals to the front.

Although we were among the first units in town, we missed the entire show. We were well down the road by the time the "big find" hit the newspapers.

U. S. Army Signal Corps Photo, Courtesy National Archives

In charge of the salvage operation, Colonel Bernard Bernstein examines suitcases full of items looted from civilians – April 1945.

Ever Eastward!

We continued to roll through eastern Germany at breakneck speed. One town fell after another, with little opposition. We soon hit a section of the German Autobahn, which most likely connected Berlin with Nurnberg with Munich. A veritable hodgepodge of different enemy outfits sped down the road, destination anywhere but there. We mixed it up with most all of them and collected a significant amount of POWs.

U. S. Army Signal Corps Photo, Courtesy National Archives

Ever eastward, 90th Division troopers attack a German village along the Saale River – April 1945.

Next, we assaulted the much larger city of Hof, Germany. Bombs had pasted her outskirts into ruble. Yet, the resistance proved immediate and formidable. From the outset, we staged a house-by-house brawl.

German snipers caused considerable problems. With so many houses and buildings, hiding places were plentiful. Each city block contained a ready supply of concealed enemy marksmen. American riflemen often relied on machine gunners to silence the most troublesome targets.

239

U. S. Army Signal Corps Photo, Courtesy National Archives

*On the streets of Hof, a 90th Division jeep
passes by a burnt-out Nazi vehicle – April 1945.*

U. S. Army Signal Corps Photo, Courtesy National Archives

*3rd Battalion, 358th Infantry riflemen look-on as M
Company machine-gunners eliminate enemy sniper
positions in Hof, Germany – April 1945.*

From early afternoon, throughout the night, deep into the next day, we fought for Hof. We secured her streets, block by block. In the process, we collected 825 prisoners, plus another 4,000 wounded enemy soldiers at the local hospital.[10] It was one hell of a battle, but Hof eventually fell.

U. S. Army Signal Corps Photo, Courtesy National Archives

90th Division troopers push through Hof, Germany – April 1945.

Window Shopping At Hof

Although her outer reaches lay in ruins, portions of the downtown area were amazingly intact. A population center like Hof offered many badly needed items to a rag-tag bunch such as ours. Once the scene was secure, most of us went window-shopping.

A buddy from Thermopolis, Wyoming, Elijah "Sonny" Dodge and I scoured the city together. An upscale clothing shop caught our attention. Trimmed in black glass, the storefront was very well done. Sonny and I had only recently discussed our need for some new T-shirts. Terribly worn, ours more resembled window screens than clothing.

Elijah "Sonny" Dodge
M Company, 358th Infantry

Sonny tried the door, but found it locked. Rather than simply break the glass, a bazooka team from across the street offered to open her up for business. With two shots, they blew in the entire storefront. We sorted through the tangle to find box after box of new T-shirts. There were so many that we began to throw them out into the street, which attracted quite a crowd. Dirty GIs from all over town partook in the spree. One article of clean clothing could make a grunt's day.

Hot Bath, Anyone?

Still together, Dodge and I searched for a place to wash up. The first house we toured was both empty and clean—all that we needed, and so much more. From the corner of the upstairs bathroom, a coal-fired stove functioned as a water heater. We first got that thing roaring full blast, then filled the tub with water. While Dodge scrubbed and soaked, I sprawled out on a bed. A clean T-shirt and a soft place to lay my head, with a bath on the way—I could get used to Hof.

You just can't imagine the grime that one body can accumulate. I drained Dodge's aftermath, which closely resembled a mud puddle, then filled the tub for myself. I basked in the hot, sweetly scented water, lathered and rinsed several times to take full advantage of the fragrant soaps and bath crystals. Oh, what a feeling! In one hour, I made up for months of hygiene neglect.

Lifted by the combination of a bath and a new T-shirt, my spirit soared. I got dressed, then woke Dodge from his nap. Two squeaky clean GIs, with a little more bounce in their step, rejoined their unit. We left Hof and a lot of personal filth behind.

Humanity At Its Worst

The 90th Division rolled south along the line between Germany and Czechoslovakia. We manned the left flank. On April 18, 1945, Division Headquarters sent a small outfit, which included machine gunners from "M," across the border. The move distinguished our group as the first to completely traverse Germany, from west to east.[11] We had sliced through the center to cut the country in two.

It seemed more for show than anything else. The squad soon returned and we resumed our march southeast, on the German side of the border.

Days later, we happened on a scene that none of us would ever forget—the Flossenburg Concentration Camp. Portions of Patton's 3rd Army liberated the facility on April 23, 1945.[12] Forward units of the 90th and 97th Divisions were the first to arrive.

U. S. Army Signal Corps Photo, Courtesy National Archives

View looking down into the Flossenburg Concentration Camp – April 1945.

It stung in that there had been days, although few and far between, when I'd actually felt sorry for the Krauts— like those anti-aircraft gunners at Mainz, literally burned alive. But as we moved farther east and continued to unmask the Nazi prison and labor camps, my heart soured. After witnessing the carnage at Flossenburg, I raged with hate.

I still find myself at a loss for words to describe it. Terms like "war crimes" or "atrocities" fall short. They're too sterile, too bookish when compared to the ghastly sights, sounds and smells of that place. Although words must suffice, they'll never do it justice. Words don't make you retch or reel away or cover your nose and mouth, but Flossenburg did.

*358th Infantrymen pause to examine a dock area, where the
dead were loaded onto trucks, bound for the crematorium.
In the final year of the war, an estimated 1400 Flossenburg
prisoners died each month from starvation alone – April 1945.*

I viewed the ovens, the bleak housing, the despicable
sanitation system, the dead and perhaps worst of all, the
living. I saw stacks of corpses. Apparently, the crematorium couldn't keep up with the brisk pace of death. Those
who survived looked like living skeletons, dead men walking.

Over the previous four years, an estimated 35 to 60
prisoners died daily, totaling nearly 100,000 lives lost.[13] In
his book, *Battalion Surgeon*, William M. McConahey
made special note of one group in particular. He wrote:

*"It should be remembered by all Americans that it was
here that 15 of our brave, gallant paratroopers were*

hanged one Christmas Eve. Their 'crime'? They had escaped from a prison camp and they were American paratroopers (whom the Krauts feared and hated). At the war crimes trial in Nurnburg it was testified that at Flossenburg Concentration Camp on Christmas Eve, December 24, 1944, 15 American paratroopers were hanged by the S.S. beside gaily decorated Christmas trees, at a sadistic 'Christmas party' for the inmates, who were compelled to watch the exhibition." [14]

U. S. Army Signal Corps Photo, Courtesy National Archives

358th Infantrymen stare in shock at an enormous pile of discarded shoes. The shoes were removed from dead prisoners before their bodies were burned – April 1945.

It was humanity at its worse, and I saw enough to last me a lifetime. But sadly, the Flossenburg facility was not where the story ended. With word of our imminent assault, camp guards and officials fled the grounds, force-marching over 10,000 inmates southeast. In a 1945 article, as reprinted in John Colby's *War From The Ground Up*, Captain James C. McNamara shed light on this sordid trek. He wrote:

"...On one pine-studded knoll outside the village of Nuenberg lay the battered bodies of 161 Polish Jews, shot and beaten to death by SS guards for faltering along the way.

"...The bodies crumpled in the roadside mud bore unmistakable signs of clubbing and shooting.

"...The exodus from the camps of brutality under the supervision of sadistic SS barbarians was a march of death where men were shot on the slightest provocation.

"...One prisoner said a man was left for dead every 10 yards of the hellish route from Flossenberg south to the village of Posing—a marching distance of 125 miles.

"...Scarcely 6,000 survivors of 11,000 men were left to greet the Americans." [15]

The fleeing German Army freely hopped over the border and entered Czechoslovakia. Up to that point, we had been letting them go. But no more—it was time to run them down and end this thing. In early May 1945, near Waldmunchen, Germany, we crossed the Czechoslovakian border en masse and surged toward checkmate.

Chapter 17

Into The Cold War

Haselbach, Czechoslovakia to Schonthal, Germany

A Warning From Above

Trucked to the city of Haselbach, we traded Germany for Czechoslovakia. We quickly debarked and marched east, through woods and ridges, parallel with a road connecting Waldmunchen, Germany and Domazlice, Czechoslovakia.[1]

As we prepared to enter another large wooded area, a low-flying Piper Cub caught our attention. Not only did those guys spot for artillery, but they also often reconnoitered ahead for infantry. They normally radioed their findings to contacts on the ground. Artillery then passed pertinent news forward to us.

That pilot was all over the place. Was he trying to tell us something—manually relay a message? Maybe his radio was inoperable. Whatever the case, we couldn't figure it out and continued on our journey.

To our amazement, he put his plane down, right on that road. Wow! We all stood a little shocked! We'd worked with Piper Cubs for a long time, but never had one land amongst us.

Sure enough, although a brand new aircraft, the radio didn't work. The pilot quickly warned us of a large concentration of German armor and infantry directly ahead. No sooner were the words out of his mouth than we hit the enemy.

We tried to turn his plane around, but the road was too tight. We literally lifted the tail and attempted to swing it, but got snagged in the bushes. It was too late! The battle was on! We shot her up and set her ablaze.

U. S. Army Signal Corps Photo, Courtesy National Archives

You can run, but you can't hide! A 90th Division, 155mm howitzer fires the first artillery rounds into Czechoslovakia - May 1945.

Our Last Fight

The forest grew thick and wild—alive with enemy soldiers. We jumped in and pushed the Germans back, tree by tree. It was too rich a confrontation for May 1945. We, as well as our enemy, knew the war was over. Yet there we were, killing each other again.

The 358th Infantry searches out a fleeing enemy force, through the densely treed forest near Klenec, Czechoslovakia - April 1945.

The weather openly objected to the hostilities. The air turned cold, then the wind picked up, whipped and howled. Soon, snow began to fall, thick and heavy. Certainly odd for that time of year, maybe Mother Nature was trying to tell us something. And if a winter storm in May was any indication, she wasn't pleased.

The day faded into night, but we still waded, waist-deep in Krauts. We backed off a bit and set up a perimeter. I don't imagine anyone slept. I know I didn't. No one wanted to die that close to the end.

At dawn, we surged forward. Much to our delight, the enemy had withdrawn under the cover of darkness. We passed clear of the forest and took to the open road.

Our battalion alone suffered 34 wounded and 6 KIAs.[2] We mourned these dead much, perhaps more than any other of the war. They had come so far, survived that long only to be killed a few short days prior to the official end. And, for what? Nothing—not a damn bit of difference! It seemed such a senseless waste of life.

Calling It Quits!

Only days later, near Vseruby, Czechoslovakia, Germany's mighty 11th Panzer Division surrendered to our division. An enemy officer, bearing a white flag and note from his commander, crossed into the 90th's ranks. The message read:

Division CP 3 May 1945
11th Panzer Division
Commander
The development of the military and political situation makes it desirable to me to avoid further losses on both sides.

I have therefore ordered the Major, the bearer of this note, to negotiate with you the cessation of hostilities.

von Wietersheim
Lt. General and Division Commander [3]

The act was huge in that the 11th Panzer Division was one of the few enemy units that remained fairly intact. At over 10,000 men strong, with hundreds of vehicles and weapons, they surely could have yet inflicted countless casualties, and prolonged the war for weeks, if not months.

90th Division troopers gather around a building in Vseruby, Czechoslovakia, where Lieutenant General von Wietersheim signs for the surrender of his 11th Panzer Division – May 1945.

In the end, a fear of the Russians no doubt impacted General von Wietersheim's timely surrender. No German wanted to be captured by the Red Army. They were almost desperate to be taken by us. Some even opted to commit suicide, rather than face an uncertain future in a Russian gulag. I can't say that I blame them.

Finally!!!!!

On the morning of May 7, 1945, Division Headquarters received the word that we'd all been awaiting. The message said:

"A representative of the German High Command signed the unconditional surrender of all German land,

sea and air forces in Europe to the Allied Expeditionary Forces and simultaneously to the Soviet High Command at 0141B Central European Time 7 May 1945 under which all forces will cease active operations at 0001B 9 May 1945."

EISENHOWER [4]

Word spread quickly throughout the ranks. It was over! I can well remember the day my war ended. I'll never forget it! Along an anonymous lane, I sat in the mud. We were at rest between route marches in the middle of nowhere, Czechoslovakia. I noticed an American jeep driving toward my position. Oddly, the crew paused every few yards to speak to the ditch dwellers and were causing quite a commotion. I stared intently, but couldn't hear what was said until they stopped in front of me.

"Hey, the war's over buddy!" the passenger announced.

"I've been waiting on you for three years!" I yelled back as they continued on down the line.

I didn't know what to think or do. No one did. A flood of emotions overwhelmed us all. A few laughed, danced and sang. Some quietly crouched, cried and prayed. Many others sat silent, numbed by the news.

We knew it would end sometime, but none of us were sure we'd see it, especially after the deaths a few short days ago. We'd been soldiers for what seemed like forever. In our year of war, fresh-faced boys became men, tempered by the worst imaginable. We lost life's innocence along the way. None would ever be the same again.

Meeting The Reds

The party was short-lived. We were soon ordered to the north. Our Red Russian allies continued to move west in an effort to grab ground, even after war's end.

Although on the same side, we admittedly knew little of each other.

We hurried along to finally meet our Soviet comrades. In World War II's waning moments, we unwittingly plunged headfirst into what would become a battle for world domination, waged planet wide over the next forty years—the Cold War. Per orders, we took up residence to block any further Russian progress west.

At first, the scene was jubilant! We greeted each other warmly! Together, we celebrated an Allied victory and an end to war. Yet, once the novelty wore off, our differences surfaced. We were fire and ice, allies with less in common than enemies.

Friends at first! Russian and American allies gather for a group photo in Kasejovice, Czechoslovakia - May 1945.
Second row, far right: Charlie Hensal.
Third row, far right: Hobert Winebrenner.
Fourth row, middle: Joe Stalin.

The situation might have proved tolerable, given space between. But we lived on top of each other, both occupying the same small burg. Neither side backed down. The close proximity caused much friction. So began our weeklong camping trip with the Red Russian Army.

First Impressions

They ranked a rough-looking lot, to say the least. Before meeting them, we thought of ourselves as the dirtiest band of hobos ever to grace Europe. Those guys beat us, hands down!

Their operations were as coarse as their appearance. They drove American-made, 2.5-ton Studebaker trucks. Most of the doors were ripped from their hinges.

They hauled their gasoline in 55-gallon drums. Whenever the need arose, they just removed the bung, tipped the barrel over and aimed for a smaller bucket. From there, they attempted to pour the fuel into the vehicle. Sometimes they used a funnel, while at other times, they did not. From the drum to the truck, I think they lost half their gas on the ground.

Not any easier on jeeps, they again drove American-made. Rather than laid down, most windshields were torn off. Rope secured many a disfigured hood. The poor things hadn't been clean since they left the boat.

Our motor pool treated their vehicles with tender loving care. A well-kept truck or jeep rated as a source of pride. They coddled them, almost like their own children. When our drivers witnessed those American-made vehicles all but destroyed in Russian hands, they took great offense. It was a little comical. We had to remind them that those things weren't living entities. I'm sure they had nightmares about suffering and tortured transportation.

Strapping On The Feed Bag

Russian mess made their vehicle maintenance look

cutting edge. That first day, several of us noticed a horse team drawing a huge, wheel-mounted, cast-iron kettle down the street. We sat at a distance to take it all in.

They pulled the big pot up to a house, then removed the horse team, gear and wheels. One group ripped apart the front porch and started a fire under the kettle. Another band searched out livestock, maybe a cow or a couple of pigs. It really didn't much matter. They brought the animals back and butchered them right there on the spot. With little attention to detail, they chopped the meat into large chunks, then tossed them into the empty pot. Cooks added several buckets of water and brought the concoction to a boil.

Others returned from scavenger hunts with whatever they happened to find—cabbages, carrots or turnips. They topped the vegetables and threw them in. The attendant grabbed a board from the porch to periodically stir the stew.

They leaned on the locals to bake their bread and forced them to fill quite a quota. The town really had to hustle to keep up.

Most of us had discarded our mess kits long ago, but kept our spoons. The Reds didn't even have that. For plates, they helped themselves to whatever the neighborhood had to offer. One might eat from a pot lid, while another used a bucket found down at the barn. For utensils, a piece of bread or cupped hand seemed to suffice. When the dinner bell rang, they all passed through a line to ladle their containers full of that slop.

It was crude. After watching that once, a K-ration never looked so good. But in hindsight, I probably ate worse. And it was better than starving to death.

"No Damn Trade!"

Initially, parts of both sides occupied the same schoolhouse. It was tight, but home. On our second day there, my friend, Charlie Hensal and I walked the hallways, just to check things out.

In his late thirties, Charlie was our elder statesman. He looked the part as well. As a first-rate cowboy from Oklahoma, he'd spent years in the wind and sun. His weathered skin reminded me of leather.

Early on, his grandmother mailed his pistol to him. She also occasionally sent over watermelon-rind preserves. Although they may not sound appetizing, once you tried them, you were hooked! They were absolutely delicious, and as I've said before, anything from home was automatically better.

His gun was nothing special, just a beat-up, long-barreled .45 revolver. But it was his, and that's why he wanted it. Guys became attached to their weapons.

Charlie was a little different in that he never cared for holsters. He always tucked that pistol in his belt, just behind the buckle.

At the schoolhouse that day, we crossed paths with many Russians. After all, it was their home too. Most passed by with a nod, but two young Reds confronted us, stopped us in our tracks. One noticed Charlie's weapon and desired a closer look. Brazenly, he pulled it from Charlie's belt, completely unannounced. It caught us both by surprise. He quickly examined Charlie's revolver, then reached into his own holster to remove a nondescript, punch press .38. Without so much as a pause, he stuck his gun into Charlie's belt and offered, "Trade! Good!" and then hurriedly walked away.

It all happened so fast that it took some time to register. When it finally did, we followed. Charlie was understandably hot! Thankfully, they were still in the building. Charlie grabbed the Russian's wrist and turned his hand open. He slapped the .38 into it as he yanked his own .45 from the man's belt.

With authority, he proclaimed, "No damn trade! No

damn good!"

The Russian didn't like that one bit and started to make some noise. He then pushed Charlie in the chest, back a few steps. Bad move! Just that quick, Charlie drew his weapon. The two young Russians soon realized that they'd hooked horns with a cantankerous old cowboy just crazy enough to shoot them both. Thankfully, they didn't stick around for the Wild West revisited.

Bad Gets Worse

The friction only intensified. We took great offense at the manner in which some of these guys treated the locals, especially women. Word of multiple assaults spread throughout our ranks. It's true, you can't judge the whole by the acts of a few, but we'd seen enough to sour us on many.

The situation soon reached a boiling point, ready to explode into open hostilities. Sensing this, our higher-ups ordered us away. We moved our camp into the Czechoslovakian countryside.

White Russian Tragedy

While there, an entire White Russian, Cossack Cavalry unit surrendered to us—thousands of them. Because of their differences with the Reds, whether political, ethnic or both, they had fought on the side of the Germans.

They all rode horses—strictly "old-time cavalry." After years at war, the animals were bony. But our resident horse expert, Charlie Hensal assured us of their quality. The saddles were handcrafted from beautiful yellow leather.

To a man, they stood taller than the Reds. Even in the summer heat, many still carried ankle-length coats and bearskin hats. Most were armed with sabers, short-barreled carbines and submachine pistols.

Although their suffering was clearly evident, they

proved much more civilized than their communist counterparts. They were almost regal when compared to the Reds, at least in my opinion. Even though they had sided with the enemy, I favored them over our Russian allies.

They were careful to surrender to us rather than their natural enemy. They believed we'd treat them honorably, spare their lives. If the situation wasn't tense enough already, the act ratcheted things up another notch or ten.

We allowed the officers to keep their weapons, but disarmed everyone else. We stacked the saddles in a pile and pastured the horses in a nearby field. Our neighbors went wild, outraged that we would even consider protecting the "traitors!" To them, it was strictly an internal matter. To us, the Cossacks were POWs, to be treated as such—no more, no less.

The fate of those cavalrymen started climbing the chain of command. How high it eventually scaled, I don't know. But word soon arrived, "Hand the Whites over to the Reds!" Our hearts sank. Had we just signed their death warrants?

William McConahey, M.D., in his book *Battalion Surgeon*, also made note of the event. *"I watched them go by, back toward the Reds, as beaten and dejected a group as I have ever seen. I felt a little sorry for them ...I wonder if they were massacred by their Red brethen."* [5]

Their new captors trucked them away. I have no evidence of a mass execution, just my own suspicions. Perhaps they set the Cossacks free and sent them home. But, my gut tells me otherwise. Over the years, I've privately pondered whatever "officially" became of these men. Were any ever seen again or did they all just disappear? In any case, not from my mind! I can still see their faces.

I felt ashamed. I had always believed that we were the "good guys," but not on that day. I found out firsthand that the deadliest part of war was often politics. God, forgive us?

A Man And His Horses

In defiance, we kept the Cossack horses and saddles. As expected, it brought a Red uproar, but we didn't care. We almost longed for a confrontation.

General Patton, who himself was a horseman, caught wind of this rare opportunity. Although I didn't witness it myself, I heard that he surfaced to claim the pick of the herd and had the best few shipped away, perhaps to his home at Green Meadows Farm. Of course, he died before ever leaving Europe. Tragically, his wife Beatrice was killed in 1953, when thrown from a horse. I've often wondered if it could have been from one of the Cossack Cavalry steeds.

U. S. Army Signal Corps Photo, Courtesy National Archives

General George S. Patton (center), along with his entourage, awaits the arrival of General Eisenhower - Etain, France.

I admired Patton for, among other things, speaking his mind. He called it just as he saw it. At the time, he was the only one to both recognize the threat in Russia and possess the courage to publicly admit it. While our country's hierarchy appeased the Soviets by handing them Eastern Europe, Patton spoke of the dangers ahead. We knew what he was saying. We lived it everyday. Yet, I guess grunts were best seen and not heard—even the top one.

Military Government

Toward the middle of May, we backed off to the German-Czech border for occupational duties. As military government, M Company was assigned the area in and around Schonthal, Germany. Happily away from our Russian allies, we made ourselves at home.

Schonthal proved extremely hospitable. The people were very kind. They not only offered us home-cooked meals, but also quartered our horses. Small breweries operated throughout the region and were all quick to barter a bucket of beer for next to nothing, usually gum or cigarettes.

Some days, I traveled with the mess jeep, to deliver hot chow to our outposts on the border. Well into one such journey, we happened on four German farmers. Clearly excited about something, they frantically waved their hands as they raced our way.

We soon learned that three had been shot. Their wounds were not life threatening, but still a cause for great concern. After all, we were the new sheriffs in town. They explained to us that a group of former prisoners were hiding in the woods, up the way. One possessed a pistol, and was not shy about firing it at passers-by.

I directed the wounded farmers to our medical detachment at Schonthal, and then we rolled forward to address the problem. Neither the driver nor I felt good about the situation. Years of physical and mental abuse left those poor souls unpredictable at best, deadly at worst.

We inched down the lane. A densely treed forest flanked each roadside. Extremely tense, I pulled my sidearm and slid it into the top of my left boot. The driver paused to load a carbine and ran a round into the chamber. With the windshield down, he laid his weapon on the hood.

There they were. Still in their prison stripes, they casually reclined in the ditch. I hoped they were from a labor camp and not one of the nearby torture chambers, Passau or Flossenberg.

They sat on my side of the road. We stopped directly in front of them. The driver got out and leaned across the hood with his carbine shouldered and ready. I remained in the jeep. One of the crew rose and sheepishly walked to my position.

"Who has the pistol?" I asked firmly, as I mimicked a gun with my hand.

The man smiled, shook his head, shrugged his shoulders and answered in heavily accented English, "No pistol."

I looked him straight in the eyes and lifted my .45. When I tugged the hammer back, his grin was gone. He got down on his knees and switched to fragmented German in midstream, "Nicht habben! Nicht habben!"

I took aim at his forehead, extended my left hand out open and demanded, "Pistol?"

Immediately, he scampered over to a clump of moldy bedding. He pulled out a lugar and handed it to me, butt end first. We ordered them to gather up their belongings and be on their way.

I felt sorry for them. What would they discover on finally making it home—only a shell of what once was? The war had taken so much from so many, but none more so than from those folks.

Chapter 18

My Last Leg

Marseilles, France to Fort Wayne, Indiana

Going Home? Not Yet!

The point system picked and chose soldiers to ship home. With a year of combat experience plus two Purple Hearts, I assumed my total well exceeded the number required. But much to my chagrin, instead of heading stateside, I received orders for Marseilles, France. There was a new unit in town, fresh from the States, low on NCOs. I, along with several others, was sent to fill its ranks. A raw deal, if you asked us.

The group had arrived too late for the war in Europe, but was now earmarked for the invasion of Japan. Once we whipped them into fighting shape, we were suppos-edly homeward bound. Yet, none of us really believed that. We'd been around long enough to know the differ-ence between what we heard and what we saw. And what we saw was a bunch of old-timers on their way to Japan.

We didn't like it one bit! We felt like we'd done our

share of the fighting. We had walked and fought through France, Belgium, Luxembourg, Germany and into Czechoslovakia. Several of us held a handful of Purple Hearts.

But maybe even more than that, we hated being split from our units. We had grown from a collection of individuals into tight-knit families that would go anywhere or do anything for one another. If they had ordered the entire 90th Division or even whole regiments within it to Japan, they wouldn't have heard much about it. But instead, they separated, then sorted us into new outfits. Although we disagreed, we again followed orders.

Not Home, But Not Too Bad

We unfortunate ones loaded onto 2.5-ton trucks. Each pulled a trailer that carried our gear. The weather was perfect and the countryside was beautiful. Atop our packs, I soaked in the sun. It would have ranked as a wonderful trip had it not been for the invasion of Japan looming over our heads.

Our first stop was Frankfurt, where the cleanup had already begun. The city looked much improved, compared with the last time we saw her, just a few short months ago. We next halted at Nancy, France. The weather held; the sun shined throughout our journey.

A few more days travel brought us to Marseilles. Once there, we immediately split into different units. My outfit's camp sat on a slight bluff that overlooked the Mediterranean Sea. We were only walking distance away from a beautiful beach.

Instead of training for an amphibious invasion, my group guarded a huge dump of supplies and rations. My seniority brought me pick of stations. I fancied the view from a particular gate that faced the water. Throughout each day's duty, I watched the waves and dreamt of home. Four hours on and twenty off, life at Marseilles resembled vacation more than war.

Finally, Again!

In August, Japan surrendered. That was it! I'd be going home for sure! Again, it was cause for celebration and that's just what we did!

With a large port there at Marseilles, I figured I'd be on a boat in no time. Yet, that must have made too much sense. I received orders to ship out of Le Havre. I would need to traverse the entire north-south length of France to catch my ride home.

We trucked to a nearby depot where we loaded onto boxcar after boxcar, forty men per, plus six bales of straw. Now that's riding in style! For the three-day trip, Supply issued nine K-rations to each of us.

The planners apparently forgot that France had just come through a war and its rail system lay in shambles. It took us nearly a week to trek to Paris. Everywhere we rolled, crews worked on the tracks. We often waited all day to ride throughout the night.

Early on, we built a fire in our boxcar to heat water for coffee. The small blaze was manageable, but then the train picked up speed. The quick moving air fanned the flames. Soon, it burned out of control!

As we all readied to abandon ship, the engine began to slow for an upcoming stop. We jumped out to fill empty coffee cans with water from a nearby ditch. We doused the blaze as clouds of smoke billowed from the car, but not before the flames had consumed a significant chunk of our flooring. Rightfully, that ranked as my one and only experience with building a fire on a boxcar's wooden deck.

The Hobo Life

We quickly exhausted our meager supply of K-rations. From then, we were on our own. Each time the train stopped, we foraged for food. Most towns were extremely generous and openly offered all they had. It was not uncommon to see guys return with armfuls of French bread.

We also lacked water. Although we washed up in ditches and streams along the tracks, personal hygiene suffered immensely. Within the close confines of those boxcars, the stench became almost unbearable. By the time we hit Paris, we all proved equally ripe.

A couple more days saw us to the northern coast, where we unloaded at Le Havre. We looked like death warmed over and felt even worse. They assigned each of us to one of the "Cigarette Camps." I think mine was called "Lucky Strike."

We showered and were issued new uniforms. There wasn't anything we could do for our old ones. Beyond salvage, they stood on their own. We just threw them on the burn pile.

Oddly enough, we also received heavy, warm wool socks. It immediately brought my mind back to the Bulge. When we needed socks just like those, they instead dropped us the light, ankle-cut variety. But in the middle of summer, there they were. Damn the irony!

We funneled through various checkpoints. Officers informed us that we'd be allowed to take only one souvenir pistol home and no equipment other than our government-issue uniforms. Everything else was to be turned into Headquarters.

At that time, I carried a doctor's satchel full of German pistols, a relatively new carbine and also a .45-caliber sidearm. I surely hated to part with them, but nothing was going to delay my return home. Turning them in wasn't an option. By then, I'd taken enough orders to last me a lifetime and the very word "Headquarters" rubbed me the wrong way. Down the street, I found a dugout latrine and just dumped them all in.

All Aboard!

Leaving Le Havre was monumental. Each new day brought me one step closer to home. Was it really going to happen? For the first time in a year, the odds were in my favor.

Once on the open ocean, we lined up in the payroll area, not only to collect on wages earned, but also to convert our French francs and Deutsche marks into dollars. After insurance, I think I was drawing $21 pay per month. But, I held quite a bit in foreign cash.

Ready currency soon flooded the ship, which spawned an abundance of gambling stations. Guys set up card and dice games on deck. Several scam artists got rich. I recall a few so successful that they needed bags to haul their loot around.

But, audacious winnings made for bad business. With winners came losers. And with losers came sore feelings, especially for those who felt cheated. Many men were still in war mode. I remember a couple of the boldest sharks missing roll call. Rumors circulated, but nothing concrete. Perhaps, they now worked their craft from Davey Jones's Locker.

Batten Down The Hatches

The ride was actually smooth. That is, right up until we closed in on the U.S. coastline. In a head-on collision, we faced off with a terrible storm. Churning walls of waves hoisted our troop ship up and out of the water. As the peaks rolled on, we slapped violently to the bottom of each valley. Our vessel vibrated throughout. Up and down we bobbed, over and over again, to the point that we worried our boat might break in two. I cowered below deck to hold on for dear life!

Whether we forced our way through or the storm mercifully moved farther out to sea, we finally found calmer waters. We soon cruised into Boston Harbor. The sight of American soil sent a chill down my spine. Home, at last!

We debarked and were sorted at Camp Miles Standish. It was time to say goodbye. We all wanted to get home. Amid tears and laughter, we hugged, shook hands and promised to see each other soon. Many, I'd never meet again.

A Sight For Sore Eyes

I received tickets to Camp Atterbury, Indiana. I spent a day or two there, to secure my final discharge. When I walked from that building, a huge weight was lifted from my shoulders. I was alive, free and on the last leg of my journey.

An industrious young cabby was hanging around, just outside the barracks. He was offering rides to the bus depot at a few bucks a head. The price was steep, but acceptable, considering the circumstances. There were so many of us that we could only fit a single bag per man. I carried two at the time, but didn't hesitate in discarding one. Nothing was going to slow me down.

At the terminal, I boarded a bus to Fort Wayne. Once there, I walked to my uncle's house. He lived in the city. What a feeling to stroll down those streets, blue sky above my head, birds chirping in the trees. I breathed it all in! It felt like heaven!

It was such a different world from the one I'd been living in. No ruble! No shooting! No dead bodies! At times, I had wondered if it still existed. Now I could see that it did, and just as I'd left it. Home had waited on me!

It was great to see my uncle, but there was someone else on my mind. I borrowed his car and drove down to St. Joseph's Hospital. My girlfriend, Marian was by that time a nurse. What a sight for sore eyes! When I saw her, I knew my war was finally over. My ordeal had ended. I was home again.

*The soldier and
the nurse,
Hobert and Marian,
together again!*

Afterword
(After War)

Arthur, Simon

On a vacation west, decades after the war, I tried to look up my old Indian friend, Simon Arthur. I took a chance that he might still live in the same area. I believe the town's name was Arapahoe, on the Wind River Indian Reservation of Wyoming.

With my wife Marian by my side, we drove down a dusty, windswept street. I noticed a group of young men, gathered at the corner and pulled along side for directions.

"Who are you and what do you want?" they all seemed to be asking.

"I'm looking for an old war buddy, Simon Arthur," I offered squarely.

Their expressions of suspicion changed immediately. In learning of my intentions, they quickly sent me on my way to his house.

I knew it was Simon as soon as he opened the door, but at first, he didn't recognize me. After all, it had been over twenty years, and he wasn't expecting me.

"Are you from the Agency?" he barked.

"No, I'm from Indiana," I replied.

With that bit of information, he worked my face through his memory. "Parlez vous Francais?" he asked with the hint of a smile.

"Nine, ich spreche Deutsche." I answered as we both laughed openly.

"My old friend, Sergeant Winebrenner!" he loudly announced. "Come on in!"

Simon Arthur

Simon sat on the couch, while I squatted along one wall. We talked for hours about the old and the new. After the war, he had married a Northern Cheyenne from near Birney, Montana. Together, they raised an enormous family. I think their children numbered somewhere safely in the teens.

Several things still come to mind about my visit. Above

his television hung the largest picture of John F. Kennedy I'd ever seen in my life. It was clear that he still hunted, although no longer Germans. Multiple rabbit skins dried behind the house. For a living, he worked construction and hauled local produce, among other things. I also remember him talking of trouble with the Indian Agency, regarding the education of his children. Simon was always proud of his heritage and wanted to pass that onto the next generation.

As we bid farewell and drove away, that was the last I ever saw of my old friend. He passed away in 1977, from a heart attack, while battling pneumonia.[1] I couldn't help but cry, when I got the news.

Bealke, J.W.

All who had the good fortune to serve with Colonel Bealke urged him to continue his military employment after war's end. Some men were born to be soldiers. It seemed to be his calling. He soon after accepted a commission in the regular army and made a career of it.

In retirement, he and his wife Miriam moved to Sun City, Arizona. There he died in May 1977. He is buried in Arlington National Cemetery.[2]

Benedict, Donald

Following the war, Don returned to Idaho. He chose to farm instead of teach school, and was quite successful. In 1958, he opened a feed mill and store. In 1990, he sold out and retired.[3]

Bulger, Doctor Richard

After the war, Doc moved his family to New Enterprise, Pennsylvania, and set up a family practice. Although the early years were a struggle, through perseverance and hard work, he and his wife/nurse/bookkeeper/confidant, Theresa succeeded. From "womb to tomb," Bulger doctored the citizens of New Enterprise for over forty years.

Doc was also active in his community and served a lengthy stay as the local school board president. Throughout the years, he handed diplomas to each high school graduate, many of which he had personally delivered into this world as newborn babes.[4]

Doctor Richard Bulger

Dodge, Elijah "Sonny"

While on our aforementioned trip west, we also stopped in to see Dodge. He lived in Thermopolis, Wyoming, where he owned and operated the Wigwam Bakery.

Before leaving Indiana, I purchased a new rifle, a 30/30-lever action. Just in case I got the unlikely chance to stalk some big game, I threw it in the trunk. While staying at Dodge's house, he offered to take me deer hunting. The next morning, we headed out, joined by a neighbor kid. Where exactly we went, I'm not sure. A very narrow and secluded lane led us to a remote location. We walked for a time, then spotted three deer. They calmly grazed in an alfalfa field. I'd only shot the weapon a couple of times and hadn't even zeroed in the sights. A buck stood tallest. I aimed slightly above his head and fired. The shell struck him right between the eyes to drop him instantly.

Elijah "Sonny" Dodge

While Sonny went to get the vehicle, the neighbor kid and I retrieved the deer. It was too heavy to carry all that way, so we gutted it out in this field. By the time we made it back to the lane, an Indian waited.

"Indian land!" he said, pointing to the alfalfa field from which we came. "The deer is mine!"

I just kind of shrugged my shoulders, not knowing where we were or what to do. Thankfully, Sonny soon returned. He argued that the field in question was in fact, his friend's, and that "Indian land" began at some other point.

They went back and forth for a time. At first, the discussion centered on boundaries and the deer. But gradually, the talk moved into other areas, such as their families and folks they knew in common. Before long, they reminisced like old friends. Although I never did find out whose land it was, we left with the deer. I brought it back to Indiana.

I had the pleasure of seeing Sonny several times after the war, always puffing on his pipe. Yet sadly, he too is now gone. Dodge died in 1988.[5]

Hartwick, Amon

Hit badly by 88 shrapnel in Normandy, Hartwick shipped back to the States. The severity of his wounds forced a lengthy recovery period, eighteen months in an Alabama hospital. The same steel plate, inserted in the 1940s, still holds his ulna bone together.

Amon Hartwick

When released, Amon returned to Arkansas. He worked in the grocery business, first as a market manager for Kroger. He then purchased his own store in England, Arkansas. He doubled its size and built it into the number one IGA Foodliner in the state. Now retired from the grocery game, he still works part-time as a realtor.[6]

Post war, Amon and I reunited on several occasions, including a St. Louis Reunion where we paid a surprise visit to our old Fort Sill buddy, Bill Adams. We remain close yet today.

Hensal, Charlie

Unfortunately, after we split from our occupational duties in Schonthal, I never saw Charlie again. After the war, he returned to his native Oklahoma. Near Stilwell, he died in 1971.[7]

Hoesch, Andrew

Another Fort Sill buddy, Andy Hoesch was captured shortly after the Battle of the Bulge. He spent the remainder of the war in a German POW camp. Thankfully he survived, and was eventually released.

After war, he returned to the Philadelphia area, where he lived a rich full life as an accountant, husband and father. Andrew Hoesch died in 1976.[8]

Hohman, Gail

Gail hailed from Kansas. After healing from his wounds, he returned to Randolph and became the city's postmaster. Again, we stayed in touch over the years and met up at most reunions, until his passing. Hohman died in 1989.[9]

Inman, Paul

Being regular army, Inman continued his career after

war's end. He served throughout the Korean and Vietnam Wars, but thankfully, was spared further combat.

He and his family called Edmond, Oklahoma, home. Even in retirement, he longed for nothing more than to serve others. Active in the community, he greatly enjoyed cooking at charitable functions. Paul Inman died in July of 2000.[10]

M Company Vets reunite!
Left to right: Hohman, Rother, Inman.

Levaufre, Henri

No tale of our unit would be complete without mention of Henri Levaufre, who hails from Periers, France. It was the 90th Division that cleared his Normandy village of Germans in the summer of 1944. In fact, I remember him saying that his home was destroyed in the process. Since that time, he has always held a special place in his heart for "Tough 'Ombres."

The man has researched the 90th Division with unequaled passion. It's fair to say that he knows more of our history than most that served. His door has always been open to visiting vets. He's organized so many "Tough 'Ombre" tours that it's no longer possible to keep track. On my return trip in 1980, he was everywhere, for everyone, causing many to privately wonder if he slept at all. Henri Levaufre is, and always will be, one of us.

*Henri Levaufre and Hobert Winebrenner discuss
the battle for Gravelotte, France – 1980.*

Manuel, Carl

Carl returned to Fort Smith, Arkansas, after his army days were done. There he owned and operated a service station. Manuel died on August 16, 1998.[11]

Lorena and Carl Manuel

Mateyko, John

After the war, Mateyko received his education at Rutgers University. In 1957, he moved to the Chicago area, where he set up his home and business.[12]

No one from our unit, none of us, had heard anything from or about Mateyko since the war. In the mid-1990s, believing it to be now or never, I attempted to locate my old captain. I still had his wartime address from East Conemaugh, Pennsylvania, and started my search there. I stopped by his old house, but no one knew him.

On a whim, I tried the local barbershop. Not only was the barber familiar with Mateyko, but this guy's sister graduated from high school with him and was now the secretary of their class reunions. After a quick call, I left with Mateyko's address miraculously in hand.

Opening the door to his Glenview, Illinois, home, he didn't recognize me at first. It had been over fifty years. I wanted to keep him guessing, but my wife Marian couldn't take it anymore, and let it out.

Oh, what a flood of emotions! Two tough old soldiers definitely shed some tears that day. He's since visited my place in Indiana a couple of times, and we remain friends today.

McInnis, Allan

McInnis returned to Saco, Maine. After healing from his wounds, he married and raised a family. In civilian life, he worked as a rigger at the Naval Nuclear Reactor in nearby Portsmouth.[13]

Allan McInnis

Pemberton, Howard

After the war, Pemberton returned to the Columbia, Missouri, area. He farmed for a time, then got into wholesale plumbing supplies. In retirement, he splits his time between Iowa and Texas.[14]

Howard Pemberton

Rezac, Henry

Henry hailed from Dante, South Dakota, but was Czechoslovakian by ancestry. In fact, he spoke the language fluently. The hidden talent came in quite handy near war's end. While stationed in Czechoslovakia, we often leaned on his ability to communicate with the locals.

He even met a girl over there! Shortly after the war, she returned to Dante with him and became his bride. Together, they raised a family, farmed several hundred acres and enjoyed many a traditional goose dinner. Henry Rezac died in 1985.[15]

Rother, Paul

Following his soldiering days, Rother returned to Okarche, Oklahoma. While he and his wife raised nine children, he owned and operated two Culligan dealerships. Paul died in April 2002.[16]

Winebrenner, Hobert

I came back to Merriam, Indiana, and married my wife Marian. We soon after built a modest home, which we've lived in ever since. We raised two sons and a daughter, Steve, Tony and Jane Ann.

For a living, I returned to GE in Fort Wayne, where I was a welder and a maintenance man. I retired in the early 1980s, after forty years of service.

Hobert and Marian Winebrenner

Final Thoughts

It's always been there. Even though with the Lord's blessing, I've moved on to live a wonderful life, the war has always remained with me. Most days, it resides in the back of my mind, while on others, it surges to the fore-front. It's not necessarily something I've tried to escape, but rather, something I've learned to live with.

It's part of who I am. Not so much physically, but maybe even more so. The war helped shape my charac-ter and mold my being. Through it, I gained perspective. When you've been at the bottom, everything else is up.

Politicians called the shots. Generals made the moves. But, soldiers fought the war. I think of those who didn't come home—friends like Marsh, Rogers, McHolland, Masters, Roeglin, and the list goes on and on. It's been sixty years, but I can still see their faces, hear their voic-es. I wonder, does anyone else think of them? Do their communities know their names and what they did? Or, has it all been forgotten?

I sincerely hope that each one carries on in the lives they touched, before offering the ultimate sacrifice for God, country and world. May we never forget these men—the finest I ever knew, and what they did for us all?

I wrote this for my family—my children, grandchildren and great grandchildren, so that they might know of our fight for freedom, even after all of us have gone. At eighty-two years of age, as my time too draws near, I stand ready. I do not fear the future, but look forward to the life beyond and catching up with some old friends. I sincerely hope that you've found this walk in my *Bootprints* to be worth your time. Thanks for reading.

Endnotes

Chapter 1
1. Telephone interviews with Amon Hartwick, 2003.
2. Lieutenant Colonel Charles B. Bryan, *Battle History Third Battalion 358th Infantry* (Plzen, Czechoslovakia: Novy Vsetisk, 1945), 9.

Chapter 2
1. Letter from Jane Bulger, 3 November 2003.

Chapter 3
1. Letter from John Marsh, Jr., 20 November 2003.

Chapter 4
1. Letter from Donald Benedict, 5 February 1991.
2. Telephone interviews with Donald Benedict, 2003.
3. Telephone interviews, Hartwick.
4. Telephone interview with Harold Wooderson, November 2003.
5. Telephone interviews, Hartwick.
6. Bryan, 15.

Chapter 6
1. Telephone interviews with Allan McInnis, 2003.
2. Email from Harrison County Historical Society, 16 October 2003.
3. "June Strength-Casualty-Replacement Report," *Headquarters 358th Infantry – APO 90, U.S. Army*, 10 August 1944.

Chapter 8
1. Telephone interviews with John Mateyko, 2003.
2. Bryan, 98-99.

3. Letter from Eveline Simpson, 2003.
4. Telephone interviews with Eveline Simpson and Helen Kutach, 2003.
5. Letter from Simpson.
6. First Lieutenant Joe I. Abrams, *A History of the 90th Division in World War II* (Baton Rouge, Louisiana: Army and Navy Publishing Company, 1946), 14-15.
7. Bryan, 56.
8. Bryan, 87-88.
9. Letter from Colonel J.W. Bealke to his son-in-law, John, 18 December 1975.
10. Email from Gretchen Bacon, 23 October 2003.
11. Bryan, 75-76.
12. "Daily Battalion Strength Reports," *Unit Journal, Headquarters 3rd Battalion - 358th Infantry*, 10 July 1944 and 13 July 1944.
13. Telephone interviews with Ruth Hohman, 2003.
14. Bryan, 84-85.
15. Letter from Marsh.
16. Telephone interviews with Wade Inman, 2003.
17. Letter from Marsh.
18. Telephone interviews, Inman.
19. Telephone interviews with John Marsh, Jr., 2004.
20. Max Hastings, *Overlord, D-Day and the Battle For Normandy* (New York: Simon and Schuster, 1984), 246.

Chapter 9

1. Bryan, 27.
2. John Colby, *War From the Ground Up* (Austin, Texas: Nortex Press, 1991), 171.
3. Bryan, 27-28.
4. Letter from Jerry Wiley, 25 October 2003.
5. Telephone interviews, Mateyko.

Chapter 10

1. Colby, 214.
2. Abrams, 22.
3. "Letter From Eisenhower," *Daily Regimental History - 358th Infantry*, 14 August 1944.
4. Telephone interviews, McInnis.
5. Telephone interviews, Mateyko.
6. Telephone interviews, Mateyko.
7. Letter from Bulger.
8. Letter from Bulger.
9. Abrams, 24.
10. Colby, 217.

Endnotes

Chapter 11
1. Bryan, 34.
2. Hugh M. Cole, *The Lorraine Campaign* (Washington D.C.: Historical Division United States Army, 1950), 419.
3. Bryan, 34-35.

Chapter 12
1. *Daily Regimental History - 358th Infantry*, 1 November 1944.
2. Bryan, 36.
3. Cole, 386.
4. Telephone interviews, Mateyko.
5. *Daily Regimental History - 358th Infantry*, 10 November 1944, 1.
6. Cole, 393.
7. *Daily Regimental History - 358th Infantry*, 10 November 1944, 1.
8. *Unit Journal, Headquarters 3rd Battalion - 358th Infantry*, 10 November 1944.
9. Bryan, 82.
10. *Daily Regimental History - 358th Infantry*, 11 November 1944, 1.
11. *Unit Journal, Headquarters 3rd Battalion - 358th Infantry*, 12 November 1944.
12. Bryan, 98.
13. Bryan, 81-82.
14. Cole, 496-497.
15. Telephone interviews with Howard Pemberton, 2004.
16. Telephone interviews, Pemberton.
17. Cole, 497.
18. Telephone interviews, Pemberton.
19. Letter from Howard Pemberton, 24 February 2004.
20. Bryan, 98.
21. *Daily Regimental History - 358th Infantry*, 25 November 1944, 2.
22. Letter from Wiley.
23. "Captain's Awards Are Presented To Nephews Sunday," *Springfield News-Leader*, 1 December 1945.
24. Letter from Wiley.
25. Mary Scott Hair, "Rosary For Remembrance," *Congressional Record*, 21 May 1946, A2996-A2997.
26. Hair, A2996-A2997.
27. Hair, A2996-A2997.
28. Bryan, 43.
29. Abrams, 40.
30. "November Strength-Casualty-Replacement Report,"

Headquarters 358th Infantry – APO 90, U.S. Army, 1
December 1944.

Chapter 13
1. Bryan, 44.
2. Telephone interviews, Pemberton.
3. "Citation For Silver Star," Hobert Winebrenner, 5 July 1945.
4. Telephone interviews, McInnis.
5. Cole, 589.

Chapter 14
1. Letter from Donald Benedict, 13 December 1990.
2. Letter from Donald Benedict, 1 November 2003.
3. Letter from Donald Benedict, 5 January 1945.
4. Bryan, 49.
5. Telephone interviews, McInnis.
6. *Daily Regimental History - 358th Infantry*, 31 January
    1945, 38.

Chapter 15
1. Bryan, 98.
2. Telephone interviews, Pemberton.
3. Colby, 527.
4. Bryan, 55.
5. Bryan, 83.
6. Bryan, 59.

Chapter 16
1. Bryan, 59.
2. Bryan, 60.
3. Bryan, 60.
4. Bryan, 60-61.
5. Telephone interviews, Inman.
6. John A. Busterud, *Below The Salt* (USA: Xlibris
    Corporation, 2001), 113.
7. Abrams, 79.
8. Busterud, 136.
9. George S. Patton, Jr., *War As I Knew It* (Boston,
    Massachusetts: Houghton Mifflin Company, 1947), 292.
10. Bryan, 63.
11. "Patrol In Jeeps First To Cross Czech Border," clipping
    from unknown newspaper, April 18, 1945.
12. Bryan, 64.
13. William M. McConahey, M.D., *Battalion Surgeon*
    (Rochester, Minnesota: published privately, 1966), 144.
14. McConahey, 144.

15. Captain James C. McNamara, "6000 Faltering Marchers Shot On Nazi Trek," *Sniper*, 1945. (as reprinted in Colby, 463-464.)

Chapter 17
1. Bryan, 65.
2. *Unit Journal, Headquarters 3rd Battalion - 358th Infantry*, 30 April 1945.
3. Abrams, 81-83.
4. Abrams, 83-84.
5. McConahey, 154.

Afterword
1. Telephone interviews with Mike Arthur, 2003.
2. Telephone interviews with Gretchen Bacon, 2003.
3. Letter from Donald Benedict, 5 February 1991.
4. Letter from Bulger.
5. Telephone interviews with Sandra Kerr, 2003.
6. Telephone interviews, Hartwick.
7. "County Man is Found Dead in Rural Home," clipping from Stilwell, Oklahoma newspaper, 1971.
8. Telephone interview with Mary Hoesch, 2003.
9. Telephone interviews, Hohman.
10. Telephone interviews, Inman.
11. "Carl Manuel Obituary," clipping from Fort Smith, Arkansas newspaper, 19 August 1998.
12. Telephone interviews, Mateyko.
13. Telephone interviews, McInnis.
14. Telephone interviews, Pemberton.
15. Telephone interview with Ernie Rezac, 2003.
16. Telephone interview with Naomi Rother, 2003.

Photo Index and Credits

Photo Index

Photo Index

Photo Index

Photo Index

Index

Index

Index

Index

Index

Give *Bootprints* to your friends and relatives!

Order Form

Yes, I want _____ copies of Bootprints for $27.95 (U.S.) each.

NAME_____

ADDRESS_____

CITY/STATE/ZIP_____

TELEPHONE_____

EMAIL_____

• Payment must accompany order.

• Please allow three weeks for delivery.

Your Total

1. Book(s):___ copies at $27.95 (U.S.) each =_____

2. Sales tax: 6% of total - $1.68 per copy   =_____
        (Indiana only)

3. Shipping and handling: $4.00 (U.S.) first
book, $2.00 (U.S.) each additional copy   =_____

Your total: add lines 1-3   =_____

Please make your check payable and return to

Camp Comamajo Press
P.O. Box 212
Albion, IN 46701